How To Quit Your Job
With
Rental Properties

A Step by Step Guide to
UNLOCKING *Passive Income*
by Investing in Real Estate

DUSTIN HEINER

"Ninety percent of all millionaires become so through owning real estate." – Andrew Carnegie

ISBN: 0-9975155-1-1

ISBN-13: 978-0-9975155-1-0

To my lovely bride Melissa and my amazing children Ellie, Elias, Xander, and Faith, without you, none of this would matter. Thank you for being my inspiration and motivation.

To the Lord Jesus Christ who makes all things possible and who loves me and gave Himself up for me.

CONTENTS

DOWNLOAD THE AUDIOBOOK
AND PRINTABLE STARTER KIT FREE!

READ THIS FIRST

Just to say thank you for buying this book, we'd like to give you the full Audiobook of "How to Quit Your Job with Rental Properties" **100% FREE**

We'd also like to give you a printable PDF so you can print out the charts & tables included in the book.

DOWNLOAD FREE INSTANTLY HERE

http://www.masterpassiveincome.com/FreeAudioBook

PHASE 1 – BLUEPRINT AND PLANNING

INTRODUCTION

*"Ninety percent of all millionaires become
so through owning real estate."*
– Andrew Carnegie

Thank you and welcome to the *How To Quit Your Job With Rental Properties - A Step by Step Guide to Unlocking Passive Income by Investing in Real Estate eBook!* I want to congratulate you for deciding to change your financial future and create your own financial independence. I guarantee these next seven days are going to be exciting, challenging, and very informative for you to start your investing business. By the end of this eBook, you are going to be absolutely ready to start your investing business in rental properties.

The eBook is specifically designed for you to learn how to build your financial freedom in real estate rental properties from the ground up. This eBook is designed with five separate phases that build on top of each other. After each day, you will have action items for you to complete. It is very important that you complete each day's action items. Each day will build on itself and it would be best not to put anything off and miss important keys to your success.

Stop and ask yourself these questions:

- How would my life be if I did not need to work 40+ hours a week for someone else in order to make money to pay my bills?

- How would my life be if I never had to worry about how to pay my bills again?

- How would my life be if I could design my life the way I want to live it instead of designing my life around my job?

- What are the things I would actually do with my time if I could do whatever I wanted to do?

- Where would I choose to live if I didn't have to work to pay for my mortgage?

These are all the questions the financially rich people of the world have the ability to actually ask themselves because they have their money work for them; they do not work for their money. This is the key principle of passive income. Let's look at that one more time. Have your money work for you instead of you working for your money. It sounds easy doesn't it? It is easy once you learn from those who have already designed their life to fit them, not their job. Those people have found the amazing blessings of Master Passive Income.

To get started, you need to learn how to think like those who are already rich. By educating yourself about how to use your money to work for you, you will have the ability to design your life the way you want to live it because you design your life around you, not around your job.

In order to understand what passive income through rental properties is, it would be good to understand how you can make income. There are two ways to earn income:

- Earned Income: Includes all the taxable income and wages you get from employment. i.e., working a J.O.B. (Just Over Broke) and trading hours for dollars.

- Passive Income is income received on a regular basis, with little effort required to maintain it. For example, you get paid for the value that you bring, not for the hours that you work.

> Master Passive Income - Definition: Building a real estate business that passively increases wealth, brings in monthly cash flow, and allows you to quit your J.O.B. through rental properties.

Ever wonder why the rich keep getting richer? It is because they let their money work for them rather than working for money. Ninety percent of the rich keep their money in real estate and businesses. Not only do they keep their money in real estate but keep making more from them as well. In America, the laws are not made to only benefit those who are rich since we have equal justice under the law, but the laws apply to you and me the same as they apply to the rich. The difference is the rich know how to use the laws in their favor to make more money, and you can learn how, too!

WHAT IS MASTER PASSIVE INCOME?

Passive income is making money by the things you "own" or "create." The goal is to replace your income with an income that comes in whether they do any work or not. Passive income allows you to get paid by the value you bring, not the hours you put in. If you have $3,500 in expenses per month, and your passive income is $4,000 a month, you can quit your job and design your life the way you want to live it.

The rich spend their time and money acquiring businesses, real estate, intellectual property, inventions, etc. These are things that bring in money every month for you and your family to live. There are many different types of passive income streams, but the way the rich make their money is by owning real estate that generates monthly cash flow.

> The Master Passive Income
> Business Model = The Less You
> Work, the More Money You Make.

It is very easy to learn the principles behind the master passive income and may even seem too simple, but that is the beauty of the master passive income model. The goal is to get paid for the value that you bring, not the hours that you work. With having a business in real estate rental properties you work hard in the beginning setting up the company, buying properties, and get them rented. After you have done all the work in the beginning, you let your systems take over, and the business makes money for you even if you do not work.

What Master Passive Income is Not

■ It is not trading hours for dollars. When you have a job, you put in an hour of work and get an hour's worth of wages in return. If you don't work, you don't get paid. Working a job is an example of trading hours for dollars, and it is not how the rich do it. Being a sole proprietor of any type of business is not a passive source of income. If you don't service your customers you don't get paid. You have substituted one boss for many different ones that can fire you whenever they want.

■ It is not easy and does take a lot of learning and hard work. For years, we have all been educated in the public school system and taught how to be an employee where we trade hours for dollars. It's time to learn a new way of making money for yourself and your family. You need to learn the strategy and tactics the rich use to create wealth, keep their wealth, and create even more wealth. It will take hard work, perseverance, dedication, and passion if you want to make passive income as the rich do with rental properties.

■ It does not happen quickly, nor is it a get rich quick scheme. The principle of the rich is they use their money to make more money. You may be starting out with very little to no money, but that shouldn't stop you, nor should it stop you that you don't know how to even get started. I did not let that stop me from starting, and you shouldn't either.

HOW I REPLACED MY JOB INCOME WITH PASSIVE INCOME

Rental properties allowed me to replace my income from my job in four years with a monthly passive income, and you can, too. How I started is probably similar to how you are starting: no money, decent credit, and the desire to learn how I can make money from rental properties. I spent $1,000 on a 2 day training course with a real estate "guru" in order to learn how to invest in real estate. The course was a very broad overview of real estate investing, and it had so much information that it was like drinking water out of the fire hose. After the two day course the guru made a sales pitch for $30,000 more for a week long course in Florida. I thought that was crazy; not to mention that I didn't have $30,000. Even if I did have $30,000 I wanted to use that money on buying a rental property.

The course had really good information, and it got me started down the path of investing in real estate. After taking the course, I made the conscious decision to become an investor in real estate rental properties. So I set off on my own path educating myself with everything I could get my hands on. The first priority was to educate myself with books, courses, and audio books. The quickest way for me to learn was to get practical experiences in real estate while buying my first property. The school of hard knocks was my main education, though, since I jumped into real estate fairly quickly after that first course. There are many lessons that I learned the hard way that I have incorporated into my investing business which helps me to be a better investor. These good and bad experiences have helped me to develop and hone my skills in rental property investing. Now I make twice as much as I did from my job in passive income.

To get started, I needed to figure out what it would take for me to retire from my job by objectively looking at my income AND expenses. By knowing what my expenses were, I was able to have a target income to hit if I would ever be able quit my job. To do that, I completed a budget for my family (like one you will be doing in this eBook), and that gave me the total dollar amount that I needed in order to live life without my job. The total I needed was $4,000 a month from passive income for my family to live securely without my job.

To get started, I took our savings of $17,000 and bought one property that cash flowed $350 per month. Each time I received a rent check, I saved the profit for future investing. I then took out a small note on the first property and bought two more properties that brought in a total of $600 a month for both. Now, my passive income from rental properties was a total of $950 per month with just three properties in one year! From there, I saved as much of the profits as I could and continued to buy at least three properties each year.

After 4 years, I owned 18 homes that rented for $500 a month which is $9,000 in rent per month! After expenses, the check I receive in my mailbox, for not doing any work myself, is right around $6,500. I had successfully surpassed my income of $4,000 per month and an extra $2,500 per month! This is not rocket science, nor is it something that you cannot do. It is something that anybody can do as long as they learn how to play the game like the rich play it. The laws are designed to make you rich with passive income in rental properties. Just by reading this eBook you are way ahead of me when I started and will learn from my mistakes. You are on your path to financial freedom with rental properties in real estate.

WHAT TO EXPECT IN THIS EBOOK

In this eBook there are five Phases you will be going through. Each phase builds upon itself just like a home you are going to buy as a rental.

Phase 1 is the Blueprint and Planning section of the learning process. A blueprint is the instructions on how to build a house from the ground up. Just like having instructions on how to build a house, you need to have instructions on how to invest properly and not lose money. Phase 1 will help you see the blueprint that you need to follow in order to replace your income with rental properties so you can quit your job and live the good life.

In Phase 2, you will be going through three days of "foundations" on which you will build your future financial freedom in real estate rental properties. Like the foundation of a building, your passive income investing foundation must be deep, solid, and strong. The foundation must be poured, cured, and set before you start to build the structure of your business. The work done in this phase will set the course for the rest of your life. Take the foundations very seriously and put in the work necessary to build a super solid foundation. In it you will learn about yourself, rental properties, and how the rich use real estate to create massive amounts of wealth, passive income, and financial freedom.

Phase 3 is the "structure" section. The structure you build, which sits on top of the foundation, is the frame of the business. This is the section that holds everything together and keeps the building from falling in on itself. With a strong structure, there will not be many things that will bring your building down because the structure is secure and sound. In this section, you will learn how you can quit your J.O.B. (Just Over Broke) and live off of the passive income you bring in through rental properties.

Phase 4 is the "finishing touches" section. In this section, you will focus on the details of your business and how to implement your business properly. The finishing touches are what everyone sees, admires, and wants to be a part of. When your business is like a well-built structure, you will be able to get through everything that comes in your way. With this section you will learn how to get to work on building your business for financial success.

Phase 5 is the section where you are given specific steps and action items to get started. If you follow these steps, it will not be a matter of "if" but "when" you get your first property. Be sure to follow each step because they are proven to work. If you are diligent and patient, you will have your first rental property within a couple months.

Remember, this is a working eBook, so it is designed to challenge you and help you on the path to financial freedom with rental properties. There will be a lot to learn, but you must push through each day and do the daily action items if you want to truly be able to quit your job.

THREE AMAZING THINGS PASSIVE INCOME IN RENTAL PROPERTIES GIVES YOU

There are three things that the rich have in abundance that most do not. Those who are educated as the rich are can have these three things in abundance too. Think what your life would be like if you did not have to work for a mortgage/rent, car payment, insurance, bills, etc. If you were able to bring in enough money to pay all your expenses without working a single day, you would be among those that are truly rich.

MONEY

Having passive income means having money to spend on whatever you want. Feel like buying a Porsche? Want to ski in the Alps with your five closest friends? Want a 5000 square foot home? All of these are possible for the rich because they have the money to do so. For the Porsche, the rich do not go out and buy a Porsche and pay cash. They buy an investment that brings in enough money each month to pay for the Porsche's monthly payment. Once the Porsche is paid off, the rich person owns the Porsche AND the investment that bought the Porsche which continues to bring in passive income year after year.

What would my hourly rate be for working two hours to buy one rental property that brings me $300 of monthly cash flow for years and years to come? The number is almost unquantifiable since the money created from my two hours of work will always be working for me. Not until I decide to sell the property and cash out would you be able to find my hourly rate. However, I do not believe I would ever cash out, but instead, do a 1031 exchange and purchase a property that brings me even more monthly cash flow. Even if I decide to sell the property and move the money into a better property, my original two hours gained me money from the property appreciating, and that money is still working for me in a new property that makes me more money.

TIME

The most expensive thing you can spend is your time. What and who you spend it on is your choice but with a J.O.B. (Just Over Broke), you are forced to spend 40 hours of your 168 hours a week working for a paycheck. There are not many people who want to spend their time working for someone else. You can be certain the rich do not want to spend their time doing that. Passive income in rental properties gives you time to do whatever you want, whenever you want.

Want to take a two month backpacking trip through the John Muir Trail in the Sierra Nevada Mountains? Or walk through Jerusalem, Bethlehem, and visit the garden of Gethsemane, all while being paid at the same time? Passive income from rental properties allows you to spend an indefinite amount of time doing what you choose to do, whenever you want to do it.

Through buying investments that bring in passive income each month, you will not have to work a J.O.B. ever again. When you are working a J.O.B. you are trading dollars for hours. The rich do not get paid by the hours they work but on the value they produce. Instead of working more hours, or trying to find a job that pays more, the rich buy more things that bring them money each month passively. When I buy a rental property, I work only about two hours on a deal from beginning to end and have money coming in for the rest of my life from that one property. The property managers, contractors, inspectors, etc., do all the work for me. I pay them well because I don't want to do the work, and they are more than willing to do it for me.

CONTROL

Master passive income gives you control over the things that bring in passive income and does not leave it up to chance, or someone else, to make their investment increase. When you buy a stock in a publicly traded company, you are buying into the profits and losses of that company. You, as a small shareholder in the company, have no say on what the business does or does not do. When you invest in rental properties, you control every aspect of the property and business.

Unlike stocks, where you have no control over the business, you have complete control over your real estate business. Want to increase rents? Increase the value of the property, and the customers will pay more to live there. Need to replace an AC unit and want to save money by buying a smaller unit because the original was too big? That is your choice. Want to pass on a tenant that has bad credit and prior evictions? Again, these are all in your control. You have complete control over the business and property to do as you see fit.

When you purchase properties as rentals, the best way to go is to "control" the property and not own them. You may buy your personal residence in your name, but the investment properties should be put into a company you create, like an LLC. An LLC is a Limited Liability Company that you own and control, and the LLC then owns the property. Since it is the LLC that owns the property and not you personally, if the property ever gets sued, you are not personally liable with your assets safe. Remember that you "control" the property; you do not own it.

Think far ahead, past your next few paychecks, to your retirement. What happens when you no longer are able to work for money because of old age? You may say, "I will have Social Security, a 401k, an IRA, a pension plan from my work, or even a nest egg saved up." All of these things are good in theory, but this is not how the rich make their money. You can say, "My money is working for me in my IRA or savings account." Sure. But the return is too low, you have no control, and it doesn't give you the ability to make enough money to design your life the way you want it.

I am so excited for you and the new journey you are on with passive income in real estate with rental properties. This eBook will take you step-by-step through the process of going from no properties to 20, 50, or even 300 properties. The sky is the limit for you and it only depends on how big you want to grow your business. Once you are done with this book, you will have the knowledge to create the income a rock star like you deserves!

PHASE 2 – THE FOUNDATION

PHASE 2.1: GET YOUR LIFE IN ORDER

In Phase II, you will be going through three sections on "foundations" on which you will build your future financial freedom in real estate rental properties. Let's get started!

COMMIT TO SELF-EDUCATION

> *"Today knowledge has power. It controls access to opportunity and advancement."*
> – Peter Drucker

To be like the rich, you need to think like the rich. A seed planted will not grow unless it gets the nutrients it needs from the soil around it and the correct amount of water. If the seed is sewn on rocky ground where there is not much soil, the seed may get water, but it will not get the nutrients it needs because there is little soil. If the seed is sown on a path, it will get eaten by the birds and never have a chance to start the growing process. The only way for a plant to grow is to be properly planted where it can get the nutrients it needs for it to grow, then God does the rest of the work.

Likewise, the only way for you to grow is to get the nutrients you need in order for you to grow. By educating yourself like the rich, you will gain the knowledge, wisdom, and examples you need to grow into the person you want to be. If you want to learn how to be a piano player, do you educate yourself on how to be a plumber? No, that would be crazy. To be like the rich, you need to learn from the rich. Try to find those around you who are where you want to be, and learn as much as you can from them. Find a mentor/coach, listen to podcasts, read books, etc. If you educate yourself about how to be like the rich, you will be able to design your life the way you want it and be free from having to work a job your entire life.

I recommend my blog post on the book Rich Dad, Poor Dad. This book helped me tremendously to learn how to educate myself to be wealthy. I had always thought that going to school, graduating from college, getting a good job, and retiring with a pension was the path to success. This book blew my mind and shattered everything that I knew, and I am so much better for having read it. You should get it now and read it ASAP.

IDENTIFY YOUR CURRENT
FINANCIAL SITUATION

"What a banker WILL ask for is your financial statement. Your financial statement is your report card for the real world."
– Robert Kiyosaki

Everyone has a starting point on any journey they take. Because of life experiences, some may be further along or behind than others. In order to take the first step, you need to assess where you are on the journey. Once you find your starting point, you will be able to know how to take that first step on the journey to becoming rich.

The first step in the long journey is to find out your current financial situation with the attached financial worksheet. This can be a difficult process to go through, but it is crucial because all the other steps build off of this. Your financial worksheet is the foundation you have been building built your entire life, and it is time find out how solid that foundation is. Take the time right now and complete the financial worksheet on the next page.

OMB APPROVAL NO.: 3245-0188
EXPIRATION DATE: 01/31/2018

PERSONAL FINANCIAL STATEMENT
7(a) / 504 LOANS AND SURETY BONDS

U.S. SMALL BUSINESS ADMINISTRATION   As of _____, _____

SBA uses the information required by this Form 413 as one of a number of data sources in analyzing the repayment ability and creditworthiness of an application for an SBA guaranteed 7(a) or 504 loan or a guaranteed surety.

Complete this form for: (1) each proprietor; (2) general partner; (3) managing member of a limited liability company (LLC); (4) each owner of 20% or more of the equity of the Applicant (including the assets of the owner's spouse and any minor children); and (5) any person providing a guaranty on the loan

Return completed form to:
For 7(a) loans: the lender processing the application for SBA guaranty
For 504 loans: the Certified Development Company (CDC) processing the application for SBA guaranty
For Surety Bonds: the Surety Company or Agent processing the application for surety bond guaranty

Name	Business Phone
Home Address	**Home Phone**

City, State, & Zip Code

Business Name of Applicant

ASSETS (Omit Cents)	LIABILITIES (Omit Cents)
Cash on Hand & in banks............................$ _____	Accounts Payable................................$ _____
Savings Accounts.......................................$ _____	Notes Payable to Banks and Others..........$ _____
IRA or Other Retirement Account...................$ _____	(Describe in Section 2)
(Describe in Section 5)	Installment Account (Auto)......................$ _____
Accounts & Notes Receivable.......................$ _____	Mo. Payments $ _____
(Describe in Section 5)	Installment Account (Other).....................$ _____
Life Insurance – Cash Surrender Value Only......$ _____	Mo. Payments $ _____
(Describe in Section 8)	Loan(s) Against Life Insurance.................$ _____
Stocks and Bonds.....................................$ _____	Mortgages on Real Estate......................$ _____
(Describe in Section 3)	(Describe in Section 4)
Real Estate..$ _____	Unpaid Taxes.....................................$ _____
(Describe in Section 4)	(Describe in Section 6)
Automobiles...$ _____	Other Liabilities..................................$ _____
(Describe in Section 5, and include	(Describe in Section 7)
Year/Make/Model)	Total Liabilities..................................$ _____
Other Personal Property..............................$ _____	Net Worth...$ _____
(Describe in Section 5)	
Other Assets..$ _____	**Total** $ 0 _____
(Describe in Section 5)	*Must equal total in assets column.
Total $ 0	

Section 1. Source of Income.	Contingent Liabilities
Salary...$ _____	As Endorser or Co-Maker......................$ _____
Net Investment Income................................$ _____	Legal Claims & Judgments.....................$ _____
Real Estate Income....................................$ _____	Provision for Federal Income Tax..............$ _____
Other Income (Describe below)*....................$ _____	Other Special Debt...............................$ _____

Description of Other Income in Section 1.

*Alimony or child support payments should not be disclosed in "Other Income" unless it is desired to have such payments counted toward total income.

Section 2. Notes Payable to Banks and Others. (Use attachments if necessary. Each attachment must be identified as part of this statement and signed.)

Names and Addresses of Noteholder(s)	Original Balance	Current Balance	Payment Amount	Frequency (monthly, etc.)	How Secured or Endorsed Type of Collateral

Section 3. Stocks and Bonds. (Use attachments if necessary. Each attachment must be identified as part of this statement and signed.)

Number of Shares	Name of Securities	Cost	Market Value Quotation/Exchange	Date of Quotation/Exchange	Total Value

Section 4. Real Estate Owned. (List each parcel separately. Use attachment if necessary. Each attachment must be identified as a part of this statement and signed.)

	Property A	Property B	Property C
Type of Real Estate (e.g. Primary Residence, Other Residence, Rental Property, Land, etc.)			
Address			
Date Purchased			
Original Cost			
Present Market Value			
Name & Address of Mortgage Holder			
Mortgage Account Number			
Mortgage Balance			
Amount of Payment per Month/Year			
Status of Mortgage			

Section 5. Other Personal Property and Other Assets. (Describe, and, if any is pledged as security, state name and address of lien holder, amount of lien, terms of payment and, if delinquent, describe delinquency.)

Section 6. Unpaid Taxes. (Describe in detail as to type, to whom payable, when due, amount, and to what property, if any, a tax lien attaches.)

Section 7. Other Liabilities. (Describe in detail.)

CREATE A BUDGET TO SAVE FOR FUTURE INVESTING

"We must consult our means rather
than our wishes."
– George Washington

Creating and sticking to a budget for you and your family is an extremely important practice that you must implement into your life. Without a budget, you will wonder where your money went at the end of the month. You don't want to be in a place where there is more month left at the end of the money. By creating a budget, you tell your dollars what they are to be used for AND you are able to plan how much you can save for future investing. They say that cash is king, and in the investing world, it is even truer than ever.

When you are creating your budget, be specific and be accurate. The more accurate you are with the numbers, the more likely you will be able to stay on budget and begin saving money for future investing. Also, you may find that you may be over spending in some areas and are possibly going into debt by your spending. Cut out wasted spending with a passion. Your goal should be to save 10% of your income for future investing. See my post on the book Richest Man in Babylon for a very good understanding of time tested ways of how to be rich.

Quick Budget

What's coming in this month (Income)

Item	Amount
Estimated monthly net income	$4.000,00
Income from other sources	$150,00
Social Security/Pension	$0,00
Total Monthly Income	$4.150,00

Am I making or losing money?

Item	Amount
Monthly income	$4.150,00
Monthly expenses	$3.420,00
Difference	$730,00

What's going out this month (Expenses)

Item	Amount
Rent	$1.550,00
Utilities	$200,00
Cell phone	$90,00
Groceries	$500,00
Auto expenses	$500,00
Student loans	$0,00
Other Loans	$100,00
Credit cards	$150,00
Insurance	$100,00
Laundry	$30,00
Hair cuts	$50,00
Medical expenses	$0,00
Entertainment	$100,00
Miscellaneous	$50,00
Total Monthly Expenses	$3.420,00

Taking Action for Phase 2.1

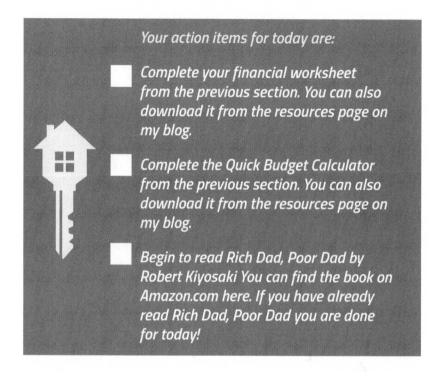

Your action items for today are:

☐ *Complete your financial worksheet from the previous section. You can also download it from the resources page on my blog.*

☐ *Complete the Quick Budget Calculator from the previous section. You can also download it from the resources page on my blog.*

☐ *Begin to read Rich Dad, Poor Dad by Robert Kiyosaki You can find the book on Amazon.com here. If you have already read Rich Dad, Poor Dad you are done for today!*

You have just completed Phase 2.1. It is crucial that you complete the action items each day and not let things slip buy. This eBook is designed to take you set by step, from beginning to end, with the goal of gaining financial freedom in real estate rental properties. By knowing where you are in the marathon of life, you now have a head start and can pick up speed fast.

PHASE 2.2: WHY YOU SHOULD INVEST IN RENTAL PROPERTIES

I n this phase, you are going to learn why Real Estate Rental Properties are the best investment for your money. Compared to stocks, mutual funds, bonds, savings accounts, etc, these and other reasons are why you must start investing in rental properties now. Let's get started!

FOUR WAYS RENTAL PROPERTIES MAKE YOU MONEY:

1. Cash flow from monthly rent

When you buy your rental properties, you must buy them in such a way that you earn cash flow from day one. The rent minus expenses is your cash flow for the property. It is not uncommon to have anywhere from $200-$300 in monthly cash flow from each property you own. It is as easy as doing math you learned in elementary school. If you buy a rental property that has a monthly rent amount of $1,100, and the total expenses are $800, you profit $300 each month the properties rented.

2. Equity!

You MAKE your money on a real estate purchase when you BUY the house. You REALIZE the money when you SELL it. Buy low, sell high.

Just as you buy the property to earn cash flow from day one, you also want to buy the property below market value, so you automatically gain equity on the property. If a three bedroom, two bath, single family home market value is $120,000 and you buy it for $100,000, you automatically gain $20,000 in equity for the property.

You, as an investor, want to get paid for the value that you bring, not the hours that you work. To build up equity yourself, you can find the worst house in the best neighborhood, fix it up with minor repairs like paint, carpet, etc., and make the value of the home increase beyond the current market value. The same $120,000 home that you bought for $100,000 will be worth $140,000 after you fix up the property and make it worth more. Also, when you build the value, the rental income goes up because the property demands a higher rent due to the superior property compared to the others for rent in the area.

3. Market appreciation

For the last 200 years, the real estate market has doubled in value every 20 years. Two of the main reasons for this are inflation and interest rates. The value of the dollar is reflected in the current gold price. An ounce of gold is worth the same 200 years ago as it is now. It is just the way in which we buy the gold that has changed in value. The dollar, through inflation, has lost its buying power over the years because of inflation. More recently quantitative easing (governments' term for printing money out of thin air with nothing backing the value of it) was implemented in order to attempt to stimulate the economy. With inflation, the homes you buy will increase in dollar value and history shows the value doubles every 20 years.

Interest rates are also a cause for price fluctuations in the real estate market. As interest rates lower, which we have seen in the past 10 years, prices go up because the ability to borrow money is cheap (currently 3%-4% interest rate), and people can buy more expensive homes for less money each month out of their pocket. If people can only afford a $1,500 a month mortgage payment, a $400,000 home at 4% interest for 30 years is a home they can afford. But if the interest is at 9% (as it was in the '80s and '90s) for 30 years, their $1,500 a month will only allow them to buy a $235,000 home.

4. Tax Deductions

Depreciation–The IRS lets you deduct the value of the property over 27.5 years. Depreciation is looked at as an expense, but no money was ever spent. You purchased the property, which makes you money and still has its actual value, and the IRS lets you deduct part of the value of the property over 27.5 years. Another great thing about depreciation is that if you give the property to your children, they get to start the entire depreciation cycle of 27.5 years all over again at the current market value!

Since Real Estate is a business, your operating expenses can be deducted from your income. Mortgage interest, insurance, repairs, advertising, Property Manager, utilities, yard maintenance, losses, etc., are all items that can be deducted from your income which lowers your income liability.

Also, other ownership expenses, like property taxes, mileage, business cell phone, professional fees for accountants and lawyers, travel, convention attendance, business education, home office, etc., can all be written off in your income taxes.

THREE WAYS TO INCREASE EQUITY

There are three ways you can create equity with rental properties. Each of these are built into the system of buying right, renting the property, and getting paid for the value that you bring, not the hours that you work.

1. Reduce debt

With the monthly rent you collect each month, part of the money goes to pay the mortgage you took for the purchase of the property. A $100,000 home, which can be rented for $1,200 per month, with a 4%, 30 year mortgage is only $477 per month. That leaves $723 per month to pay the property manager and the expenses. The balance is yours to keep as passive income.

2. Make money on the first day you own the property

You make money when you buy your rental properties because, like stocks, you buy low and sell high. Your goal is to never lose money and you can only do that if you buy a house that fits our criteria that it will make you money when you buy it. Let's say you find a deal on a property that is worth $150,000, but you can buy it for $100,000. That is an instant $50,000 equity that is kept in your investment. When you want to cash out the $50,000, you can either refinance the property and get a note for the equity, or sell the property and pocket the difference. Remember, you make money when you BUY the property, not when you sell it.

3. Forced appreciation through rehab

You can increase the value of the same property you just bought for $100,000 by rehabbing it. You can remodel the kitchen and bathrooms, add fresh paint, install new flooring, fix up the front and backyard, add another room, etc. The property that had a market value of $150,000 may now be worth $200,000 even though you only spent $20,000 to fix up the property. Basically, you can make the property more attractive to future buyers by fixing it up, and that makes the value of the property increase.

NON-MONETARY REASONS TO OWN RENTAL PROPERTIES

There are many non-monetary reasons why rental properties are amazing investments. Here are 11 other reasons real estate rental properties are the best investment:

1. Complete Control Over Your Investments

Unlike stocks, where you have no control over the business, you have complete control over your real estate business. Want to increase rents? Increase the value of the property. Need to replace an AC unit and want to save money by buying a smaller unit because the original was too big? That is your choice. Want to pass on a tenant that has bad credit and prior evictions? Again, these are all in your control. You have complete control over the business and property to do as you see fit.

2. Owning Real Estate is Seen as a Business

Because owning rental properties is seen by the IRS as a business, you get many tax deductions. These deductions makes it look like your passive income is lower and because of that, you save money.

■ Depreciation – The IRS lets you deduct the value of the property over 27.5 years. Depreciation is looked at as an expense, but no money was ever spent. You purchased the property, which makes you money and still has its actual value, and the IRS lets you deduct part of the value of the property over 27.5 years.

- ☐ Another great thing about depreciation is that if you give the property to your children, they get to start the entire depreciation cycle of 27.5 years all over again at the current market value!

■ Operating expenses

- ☐ Mortgage interest, insurance, repairs, advertising, Property Manager, utilities, yard maintenance, losses, etc.

■ Ownership expenses

- ☐ Property taxes, mileage, business cell phone, professional fees for accountants and lawyers, travel, convention attendance, business education, home office, etc.

3. Taxes on Your Properties Can Be Deferred Almost Indefinitely

With real estate, you can defer the taxes you incur when you sell your property almost indefinitely. With an IRS 1031 exchange, you can exchange the property for a like-kind investment. Like-kind is real estate exchanged for more valuable real estate. Like-kind is not selling a coffee shop business in exchange for real estate. For example, you buy a single family home, sell it 10 years later, and make $50,000. Use a 1031 exchange to buy a more expensive property like another single family home that makes more income or even an apartment building! Do all this without paying any taxes today and defer them to a much later date if you decide to cash out completely.

4. No Liability, But All the Control

When you purchase properties as rentals, the best way to own the property is with a company like an LLC. You want to "control" the rental properties and not "own" them. You may buy your personal residence in your name, but the investment properties should be put into a company you create, like an LLC or an S-Corp. An LLC is a Limited Liability Company that you own and control, and the LLC then owns the property. Since it is the LLC that owns the property and not you personally, if the property ever gets sued, you are not personally liable and your assets will be safe. Remember that you "control" the property, not own it.

5. Low Volatility in the Real Estate Market

Unlike the stock market, the real estate market does not change overnight. Even if the real estate market crashes, as it did in 2007, you are able to see it coming as well as get out of the way if needed. But, no matter what happens in the market, if you learn how to buy right, you will never have to worry about another crash in the real estate market because your rent still comes in every month.

6. Making Money In An Up or Down Market

Even better, though, is if you purchase your properties right and they cash flow from day one, you will not have to worry about an up or down market. Since the mortgage is fixed at 30 years, and you have income coming in to cover the expenses, you will always make money. Rarely do rents ever go down, and actually they are always going up with inflation. In an up market, you can sell your properties and use a 1031 exchange and buy a better property with your gains. Also, in a down market, homes are cheaper, and the rent to purchase price is more in your favor.

7. Constant Demand for your Product

The product you are selling is basically a place to live for anyone. No matter what happens to the economy, people need a place to live and will be there to sign a lease with you for the property that you own. Since everyone needs a place to live, your product will never go out of style.

8. Use O.P.M. to Start Your Real Estate Rental Business with Leverage

Go ahead and ask a banker to lend you $100,000 to buy stock in Apple or Microsoft. He would laugh you out of his office. Now ask the same banker to lend the same $100,000 to you to buy a home; be ready to sign the contract. Leverage is the most widely used means to acquire rental properties because banks are so willing to lend to the right investor who knows how to manage properties.

Leveraging a property and taking on a mortgage is using other people's money to make you money. When you buy a home with all cash, your rate of return (return of money that you put into the deal) is much lower than if you use leverage.

Purchase an $80,000 home:

☐ Paying cash in the amount of $80,000 would bring you $8,400 a year income. This consists of equity capture of $18,000, appreciation of $5,000 and cash flow of $8,400 with a total return of 38% on the $80,000 you spent

☐ You use leverage and put a down payment of $8,000 for the $80,000 home which brings you $2,400 a year in income. This consists of equity capture of $16,000, equity increase from mortgage payments of $600, appreciation of $5,000 and cash flow of $2,400, which is a total return of 200% on the $8,000 you spent.

9. Hedge Against Inflation

Inflation averages about 3% per year. If you keep your money in the bank earning .01% per year in your savings account, you are losing money every day. You may be gaining a few meager dollars, but those dollars buy less and less every year. As you can see from the savings vs. inflation image to the right, your $10,000 you saved for ten years with simple interest makes you $10 in interest. After the same ten years, your original $10,000 can only buy $9,930 worth of goods. So you may gain $10 after ten years but you lose $30 because of inflation which makes a net loss of $20.04 after ten years.

Savings vs. Inflation

.01% APR Savings		3% Inflation Per Year	
Year	Balance	Year	Buying Power
1	$10,001.00	1	$9.997.00
2	$10,002.00	2	$9.994.00
3	$10,003.00	3	$9.991.00
4	$10,004.00	4	$9.987.99
5	$10,005.00	5	$9.984.99
6	$10,006.00	6	$9.981.98
7	$10,007.00	7	$9.978.98
8	$10,008.00	8	$9.975.97
9	$10,009.00	9	$9.972.96
10	$10,010.00	10	$9.969.96

10. Insure Your Investment

You can insure your rental properties against things like loss, theft, fire, and liability. Just like you cannot get a loan for stocks, ask insurance brokers to give you insurance for losses in the stock market. They would laugh at you and then kick you out of the office. If you own a rental property with a replacement value of $250,000, you can pay yearly insurance on the property of only $700 for full coverage and protect your investment. How could that get any better? Easy! Have your tenants pay for the insurance by adding it into your numbers when you purchase the property. $700 a year is $58.33 a month. When you run your numbers when you purchase a property, make sure the costs of insurance is in there so you have it covered by the rents the tenants pay.

CREATE YOUR GOALS FOR FUTURE SUCCESS

"All our dreams can come true if we have the courage to pursue them."

– Walt Disney

In America, about 3% of the population set goals for themselves. Just by making goals for yourself, you already have a head start to becoming rich. 67% of rich people set goals for themselves in life and business as opposed to 8% of the poor. By setting goals for yourself and writing them down, you are creating a roadmap to your life. Think of where you want to be in five years and start with that end in mind. Below is your primer to get yourself on the path of goal setting.

HOW TO SET YOUR GOALS

1. Have a vision for the future you want for yourself

Picture how you want your life to be in five years. That is called having a vision and being able to see what has not come to be. A vision for your life is a picture or an idea of where you want to be if you could design your life the way you want it. If you are able to create a master vision for your life, that vision is basically a destination you can strive towards.

If you wanted to go to the Grand Canyon for vacation, there would be many steps to get there. You would need to make a decision to go there, know what the destination looks like, plan the route to get there, and set goals and milestones for you journey. It also helps if you know someone who has been there before that can show you the way. You need to have a vision of where you are going with your life in order to get where you want to go.

2. Dream big – Create four big five year goals from your future vision

Your five year goal could be to quit your job, have all your expenses paid for by passive income, and be able to travel the world. Another goal could be to have your children's college fund completely funded and buy a new house. When you are setting your five year goals, try use your vision of how you want your life to be and create a roadmap to get there! Whatever you put your mind to and stay hungry trying to attain the goals you will be able to achieve them.

You could have other goals like saving $30,000 in the bank by the five year mark. It could be that in order to quit your job, you need to have some savings as a buffer for when things don't go exactly as planned. Another goal could be that you want to be the healthiest and fittest you have even been in your life in five years. These can both be quantifiable and measurable.

3. Set specific measurable goals to attain

■ The purpose of goals is to help you attain what you desire. Make it specific, like hiking Half Dome in the Yosemite National Forest, or retiring in five years.

■ If I were to have the vision of being the healthiest and fittest ever in my life I could find the basis to start from. To reach my goal, I must beat my previous benchmarks I already have for myself. Once I beat these, I have attained my goal.

4. Set goals you can achieve with maximum effort

The saying "shoot for the moon" applies well to goal setting for your life. No, you don't want to set the expectations so high you cannot ever attain them, but you want them to be high enough to where you can get off the ground AND make it as close as you can to the moon. Try to make goals that are hard for you to attain but not so hard that you cannot do it. Goals should be ones that you must continually work on in order to achieve them.

5. Set a deadline for when the five year goals must be accomplished

When you create your five year goals, put a deadline on them to be completed. It is easiest to use either the first of the year or the date that you created your list of goals. Either way, you have a fixed amount of time to accomplish your goals and it becomes more real to you. Think of it as a work deadline that you must finish. The "future" you is the boss and the "now" you is the employee.

6. Get accountable

Reaching your goals is a hard thing to do. Life's circumstances get in the way, and things happen that throw you off the path. Having someone there holding you accountable to achieving your goals is a huge kick-in-the-pants to stay on track. Find an accountability partner who is like minded in setting goals. They don't have to have the same goals, but they must be as serious as you are about having, working toward, and attaining their goals. I suggest meeting or talking to your accountability partner weekly or biweekly, checking on each other, encouraging each other, and pushing each other along toward your destination.

Taking Action for Phase 2.2:

☐ *If you are currently renting a home to live in, strongly consider buying a home to live in where you can take advantage of these awesome reasons to invest in real estate. Go to www.zillow.com and look for homes that are 3 bedroom 2 bath and 1,400 square feet in the area you want to live. The price doesn't matter at this time. We will learn how to value these properties and buy them in Phase 3.*

☐ *If you already own your home, consider two options. One, refinance your home to a lower interest rate to save you money each month for investing in rental property. Two, consider buying a new home for you to move into and rent out the current house you are living in. Use www.zillow.com to look for homes that you would like to move into as an owner occupied home. Don't worry about the price; we will get to that soon.*

You have just completed Phase 2.2! It is crucial that you complete the action items each day and not let things slip buy. This eBook is designed to take you set by step, from beginning to end, with the goal of gaining financial freedom in real estate rental properties. Now, let's continue the foundations of your new financial freedom with rental properties!

PHASE 2.3: HOW TO THINK LIKE A RICH PERSON

I n this phase, you are going to learn how you too can be rich just like Warren Buffet, Donald Trump, and Bill Gates by learning the ways that made them rich. They do not have different rules than us, they just know how to use the rules to their advantage. Let's jump on in!

NO MORE TRADING HOURS FOR DOLLARS AND STOP WORKING

Most employees feel they are worth more than they are being paid which leads to a sense of entitlement. Remember J.O.B. = Just Over Broke. If you have only one job, usually you are only able to work 40 hours a week for one employer, and your hourly wage is typically fixed unless you are on a commission. Let's look at some of the problems with trying to become rich as an employee.

1. As an employee you trade your hours for the employer's dollars, so you are stuck with whatever the employer decides to pay you. If you will not work for the pay, the employer will find someone else to do the job and pay them instead.

2. Everyone has limited time to give to a job. Attempting to work five jobs 40 hours a week at each one is physically impossible. There are not enough hours

in the week to give, and you would not have the ability to perform as your boss expects.

3. Employees are a commodity for business owners. Just like any other commodity, it is supply and demand. If you work for Google, your job skills for the position are such that very few people can do what you can do. Your wage will probably be much higher than the normal wage because there are less people who can do your job. If you work for McDonald's, you will probably be making the minimum wage because there are many others who can do the same work as you.

4. The IRS takes almost 35% of your wages from you before you can even cash your check. Then if you consider state tax and sales tax, the total taxes you could be paying as an employee can be up to 50% of your wages. Just like that, half your money is gone!

5. The biggest problem of them all is, once you stop working, you stop being paid. If you were laid off or fired from your job, how would you pay for your expenses?

TRADITIONAL EDUCATION IS TEACHING YOU HOW TO BE AN EMPLOYEE

When we are young, we are all told to go to school and get good grades. Then we are to go to college and get a degree. Once completed, we are told to go find a job and get a pension, IRA, 401k, and we will be able to stop working when we are 65 years old. Being an employee is a very honorable career, and for the majority of society this is a perfect fit for them. The government schools do not teach us how to be rich but rather how to take orders and carry them out with a defined answer from the teacher's questions. To have financial freedom, we need to educate ourselves and learn from those who are already rich.

Those who want to be rich need to educate themselves to think like the rich because the rules of life are not different for them. Some may say that the rich in America have different rules than the middle or lower classes, but that is not the case. In America, as there is equal justice under the law, there is also equal opportunity to be rich. The only way to be rich is to learn how to use the rules to play the game as the rich do. They have the same rules but they know how to use those rules to their advantage.

It has been stated that Warren Buffet, the billionaire investor, pays less in taxes than his secretary. He actually pays a lower tax rate than his secretary, which is different than total tax dollars. In 2012, Warren Buffet paid a capital gains tax rate of 17.4% and his secretary paid an income tax rate of 35.8%. They both live under the same tax laws, but Warren chooses to make his money in a way that is taxed half as much as his secretary. His secretary is using everything she learned in school to be the best secretary for her boss, but the government still takes twice as much out of her paycheck than Warren Buffet because his income is earned as passive income. Passive Income is taxed as capital gains which has a lower tax rate (17.4%) than earned income (35.8%).

Following the example of the rich, you can use the laws to your benefit as they do:

1. Pay less in taxes and keep more of their money to spend however they want

2. Invest passive streams of income with cashflow every month

3. Quit working and stop paying the outrageous income tax rates.

4. Stop trading hours for dollars

5. Your money works for you while you enjoy it's fruits

6. Financial independence

7. You can leave a legacy to your loved ones

8. The ability to give more and more to those who are in need

The reason why it seems as though the rich have it easier than you is because they have learned how to play the game and use the laws to help them get rich.

TO BE SUCCESSFUL, YOU NEED TO BE EDUCATED LIKE THE RICH

In Robert Kiyosaki's book Cashflow Quadrant he teaches the four ways people make money: Employee, Sole Proprietor, Business Owner, and Investor.

Left side of the cashflow quadrant: E's and S's

Employee – Desires job security, a steady paycheck, no financial risk, and the benefits provided by their jobs (retirement, insurance, time off, sick days, etc.). Sense of entitlement is high with the employee, and they trade hours for dollars. They also pays the highest tax rate.

Sole Proprietor – Is their own boss and are not dependent upon other people for their financial security. These include doctors, lawyers, and anyone who is self-employed. They desire independence and tend to be controlling, not trusting others to do the work as good as they can. Their income is tied directly to how much they work and if they do not work, they don't get paid. They basically "own" a job.

Right side of the cashflow quadrant: B's and I's

Business Owner – Starts businesses and hire employees to delegate as much as possible. They work "on" the business and find competent people to work "in" the business. They desire to create a business that can run on its own without them. They focus on creating systems for the business to make money without them.

Investor – Looks for ways to make their money, as well as the money of others, work for them. They desire to work less so they can spend their time however they want while not being tied down to a job. Escapes high taxes by deferring their taxes to a future date or utilizes the IRS rules to pay the lowest tax rate of all the other groups. They receive 70% of their income from investments and less than 30% from a job.

> If you want to be rich, you should jump to the B and I side of the quadrant ASAP.

The rich focus the majority of their efforts on the Business and Investor side of the Cashflow Quadrant because that is where the real wealth and money is. The good news is, if you are starting in the Employee category you can move to any of the other quadrants at any given time. It IS entirely possible to move from E to I very quickly.

1. Every dollar you invest is another employee working for you who makes more employees who do the same

2. Live wherever they want

3. Do whatever they want

4. Buy whatever they want

5. Income comes in the mail whether they work 60 hours a week or 1

6. Complete financial freedom

7. Pay lowest of all tax rates

8. Defer taxes to a future date with IRS 1031 exchanges almost indefinitely

9. No liability because corporations own everything

10. Complete control over everything because they own the corporations

11. Not dependent on anyone for their lifestyle or freedom

12. As soon as their income from investments surpass their wages, they retire

13. Not dependent on Social Security, 401K, IRA, Pension, etc.

PRACTICAL STEPS TO ACHIEVING YOUR GOALS

Start with the End in View

Dream big and create your five year goals and work backwards from there. Start with creating your five year goals. Where do you want to be? How many rental properties do you want to own? Do you want to quit your job? How much money do you want to have saved for when you quit your job? Make a list of all these five year goals.

Create one year milestones from your five year goals.

If you want to own 15 rental properties in 5 years, how would you go about doing it? You wouldn't be able to buy eight the first year right? How about starting small and as you build year after year, your momentum gains and you can do more in year five than you did in year one. See the blog post on: "How to Retire in 5 Years"

- Year one: Buy 1 rental property

- Year two: Buy 2 rental properties

- Year three: Buy 3 rental properties

- Year four: Buy 4 rental properties

- Year five: Buy 5 Rental properties

Each goal should have yearly milestones and monthly, weekly, and daily action steps for each goal. With a general five year goal, life gets in the way, and by the time you realize it, you are in the second year without any action taken on your five year plan. Now you only have four years to do what you originally had five years to accomplish. Work on your goals daily so you can successfully reach them in the time frame you set for yourself.

Create short range goals from your one year milestones.

These should be specific action steps you can take to accomplish these one year goals. If your desire is to save up $30,000 in 5 years you can do it by either cutting expenses or increasing revenue. You may cut expenses and save $6,000 per year from your salary. Or start a small service business being a handyman to increase your annual income by $6,000 dollars and save that amount.

Each yearly goal should hopefully build on itself. After time, your small service business may not be so small because of advertising, word of mouth, etc. It may be bringing in much more money which would allow you to save the $30,000 faster AND buy more properties faster. All while beating your deadline by a couple years!

Read or rewrite your goals every day.

If you can't remember your goals, how well do you think you will accomplish them? Keep your goals on the forefront of your mind so you know exactly where you are in the process, what you need to do next, where you are deficient, and how to proceed.

Spend at least 30 min every day working on your goals.

Do anything that will help you reach your goals daily. If you wait all week to take the action steps on Friday what should have been done on Tuesday, you are almost setting yourself up for failure. Get the most important things done at the start of the day, week, month, and year so you are not up against the deadline as time runs away from you.

Do your best to not move your deadline.

I'm sorry to do this to you, but imagine this scenario: You are back in your senior year of high school and the final paper/report assignment is due tomorrow morning at 9:00 am. You had all semester to research, draft, write, proof-read, and finalize the report but you put it off until the day before, and now it is crunch time. Get it done, or fail the class. Isn't it interesting that when our backs are up against the wall we are capable of doing wonderful things in almost unrealistic timelines? Remember, you set these goals for yourself, and you also set the deadline for when these goals are to be accomplished. When you move a deadline that you create for yourself a couple things happen.

- You remove your ability to hunker down and get things done as you did when you were in high school with the report deadline.
- You give yourself permission to fail.
- You set yourself up to move the deadline again, and again, and again.

Taking Action for Phase 2.3:

- [ ] *Commit to changing your way of thinking from an employee who trades dollars for hours to an investor who gets paid by the value you bring.*

- [ ] *Read my blog post on Cashflow Quadrant by Robert Kiyosaki.*

- [ ] *Get started now! If you have not done it yet, take 15 minutes to consider and write down your 5 year goals. Really think them through and get them on paper. Take another 15 minutes and figure out your yearly milestones*

You have just completed Phase 2.3 and completed the "foundations" portion of the training. You have learned a lot and I know it is a lot to take in. Take some time to reflect on your accomplishments these last few sections.

PHASE 3 – THE STRUCTURE

PHASE 3.1 MAKE YOUR MONEY WORK FOR YOU

Congratulations!! You made it to Phase 3! You are now in the "Structure" Phase of your learning about master passive income. The structure of your learning is a lot like the structure of the properties you are looking to buy. Along with a solid foundation, the structure is very important and is what holds everything together.

You are going to learn how to have your dollars be like employees, working 24 hours a day, 7 days a week, and how to quit your J.O.B. (Just Over Broke). Ready? Let's do this!

HOW TO HAVE YOUR DOLLARS BE LIKE EMPLOYEES, WORKING 24 HOURS A DAY, 7 DAYS A WEEK

Passive income in monthly cash flow through real estate is truly passive. You are not working for a J.O.B. where you clock in or out, but you are working on your own business. With real estate, property managers are my best friends. I hire the best property manager because I want the best manager looking after my properties making me the most money while I sit back and get my monthly statement in the mail with a fat rent check. My property manager does all the work, gets compensated well, and I just make money.

By owning just one single family home with tenants who pay you monthly rent to live there, you are bringing in $300-$400 a month in passive income. You buy the home once, and your house is working for you 24 hours a day, 7 days a week. Whether you are in Hawaii or camping in the mountains, your property is working hard at making you money every minute of every day. Now imagine you had 10 properties that brought in the same amount of money each month, minus expenses. This would bring you $3,000 to $4,000 a month in passive income.

Here is the general math for one property with easy round numbers:

Rental Home on 321 Main St.–Purchase Price: $100,000

Monthly Expenses	Monthly Income
Mortgage: $536 (5% note at 30 years) Taxes & Insurance: $175	Rents Collected: $1100 Net Operating Income (NOI): ($1,100-$175)=$925
Total Monthly Expenses: $711	**Total Profit (Income - Expenses): $389**

This home on 321 Main St. would bring you $389 a month in cash flow from passive income! Now, imagine you owned 10 of these properties bringing in $389 a month in passive cash flow This equates to $3,890 in your pocket every month without you doing any work since your money is doing the work. Now, imagine how your life would be if you owned 100 of these properties. Your income would be $38,900 a month in passive cash flow!

THE PLAN—HOW TO QUIT YOUR J.O.B. IN FIVE YEARS

"If you fail to plan, you are planning to fail."
–Benjamin Franklin

In order to understand what it would take for you to retire from your job, you need to know what your expenses are. By knowing your expenses, you will have a target income needed to live off of. If you have not completed the budget in day one, do so now. Find the total expenses that you have and that will give you the total dollar amount that you need in order to quit your job. The total I needed was $4,000 a month from passive income for my family and me to live securely and not need my job. Once I found my number I was able to plan out my future investing career.

Now, let's work on how you can do the same thing, too.

Step 1: Find Your Target Income Amount

From the budget you created on Day 1, write down your total monthly expenses. This is your benchmark dollar amount you must get to in order to not need a J.O.B. to pay your bills. Once you acquire enough rental properties to pay for these expenses, you really don't need a job.

Let's say that you have $3,800 in expenses every month, and you want to quit your job and have enough income to pay your mortgage, bills, travel expenses, etc.

Now, think of what it would take to attain $4,000 in monthly passive income in monthly cash flow. It could be that in the next 5 years you buy a total of 15 properties that make you $300 a month in passive income in monthly cash flow.

There are many different types of properties that will bring you this kind of return on your money. A good rule of thumb is to stick with properties that people in the market you are investing in would want to rent. I personally stay away from two bedroom homes. They are harder to rent, the prices are almost as high, and the rents are much less. I suggest sticking with a cookie-cutter type of home.

Property Type: $100,000 Single Family Home	Property Type: $40,000 Single Family Home
B or C quality home Purchase Price of $100,000 3 bedroom 2 bathroom 2 car garage 1,400+ sqft Built after 1980 Rents for $1,100	C or D quality home Purchase Price of $40,000 3 bedroom 2 bathroom 2 car garage 1,200+ sqft Built after 1950 Rents for $750

With these two types of properties, you will have a good chance of getting a good return on your money. With interest rates being at or around 3%, the expenses and the mortgage payment would be much less than the rent, and you would get passive income in cash flow each month.

To retire in 5 years with your expenses at $4,000, your yearly plan could look like this:

Year 1: Buy one single family home with $300 monthly income
Year 2: Buy two single family homes with $300 monthly income
Year 3: Buy three single family homes with $300 monthly income
Year 4: Buy four single family homes with $300 monthly income
Year 5: Buy five single family homes with $300 monthly income

At year 5, you have 15 single family homes with $300 a month coming in. That would be $4,500 a month in passive cash flow!

Imagine what you could do with $4,500 a month! You could pay your expenses and have extra money to spend on whatever you want! If you continue on that path of adding more properties to your investment portfolio, you double, triple, or even make ten times that each month! Now, you may be thinking that buying properties in that example is impossible. Believe me, it is not. I have done it, and so can you! In 6 years I bought 19 single family homes that bring in $400 a month in passive income, and I did all this while having a full time job and a full time family. If you learn how to invest in rental properties, you will have the passive income you need to reach your goals!

Right now, buying 15 properties in 5 years sounds pretty daunting but you CAN do it! There are so many different ways to purchase rental properties that you will have no is-sue with finding them. If you learn some of the advanced techniques, you can even buy them with no money out of your pocket. In the next chapters, you will learn all the steps needed to earn passive income from rental properties and quit your job!

Taking Action Phase 3.1:

Your action items for today are:

☐ *Read Richest Man in Babylon for a very good understanding of time tested ways of how to be rich.*

☐ *Go to www.zillow.com and look at surrounding areas of your city for other places to invest. Look for properties that match the criteria above. Start an Excel spreadsheet to keep track of all the properties that catch your eye and seem to meet your criteria. Keep this sheet as a record of the following characteristics of the property:*

Address

Asking price

Bedroom/bath/sqft

Rental estimate

You have just completed Phase 3.4. Remember, it is crucial that you complete the action items each day and not let things slip buy.

PHASE 3.2: UNDERSTANDING THE PROCESS OF TURNING A REAL ESTATE TRANSACTION INTO CASH FLOW

You are amazing! You made it past half of the Quit Your Job with Passive Income in Rental Properties eBook and are still going at it. Trust me, this will all pay off in the end. It is now time to learn the nuts and bolts of how a real estate transaction works. You are going to learn step by step the process you will use when you buy your first rental property. Ready? Let's Rock!

UNDERSTANDING THE PROCESS OF TURNING A REAL ESTATE TRANSACTION INTO CASH FLOW

Now we are going to look at how you buy a rental property from beginning to end step by step. The process is not complicated but there are many steps to understand and follow. It is important to follow each step and learn the process included in each one of the steps in order to not lose money on a deal. We will start from the very beginning of the process to the end where you are making money every single month with passive income from the rent received.

Here is a diagram of the process from beginning to end.

Now let's look at each one of these individually and dig deeper to what these mean.

Process of a Real Estate Transaction to Cash Flow

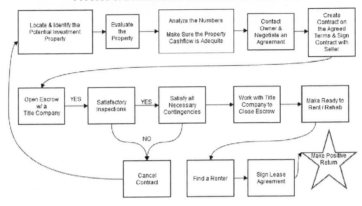

Locate and Identify the Potential Investment Property

The first step is to find a property among the hundreds that are currently listed for sale in the area where you would like to start investing. There are a few ways to start looking,but the quickest is to go to www.zillow.com and search for the type of property tthat could fit the criteria you are looking for. I suggest looking for three bedroom two bath single-family homes, with over 1400 square feet and a two-car garage. The price range should be between $80,000-$120,000. These types of properties will rent well and bring in a good cash flow each month with the current interest rate that you can get with a single family home.

Evaluate the Property

Now, single-family homes are valued based upon comparable sales in the area of like properties. So to find the value of a property you are looking at, you want to find another home within a two mile radius of the subject property that has the same amount of bedrooms, bathrooms, and square footage. By doing this you see what somebody else paid for the property and see if the asking price on your deal is a reasonable price or not. Zillow does a decent job at finding these comparable sales for you. It compares like homes to yours and gives you their opinion of what the value should be. I have found that the Zillow values are on the high end, meaning they value the property a little higher than most appraisers would.

Remember one of the reasons why we buy real estate is that we can buy a property below market value and instantly gain equity in the property. This is because we make money when we buy the property and we realize the money when we sell it. Obviously, it's best to get as much equity as you can out of the property when you buy it but that all depends on if the seller is going to sell it for less than market value. What you need to do is negotiate with the seller and try to get them to accept an offer price less than the market value. I try shoot for 80% of the market value so I instantly gain 20% equity in the property. The example below shows that if you buy a property with the market value of $120,000 for only $100,000 you will instantly make $20,000 in equity because you bought the property cheaper than what it was worth.

Market Value	$120,000
Asking Price	$118,000
Negotiated Purchase Price	$100,000
Money Made When you Bought the Property	$20,000

There are also other things that come into factor like the rehab costs which also eat into your equity because the purchase price plus the rehab costs equal the total amount to get the property rented. Your equity capture is the market value of the property minus the purchase price minus the rehab costs. If you fix up the kitchen, flooring, bathrooms, paint the walls, and do other things that make the property worth more you will increase the value of the property.

The example below shows that if you buy a home for $100,000 and you put in $25,000 to fix it up, the new market value will go up. Depending on the market the value can go up quite significantly. In this example you see the new market value is $180,000 because similar homes that are up-to-date like this one are selling for the same amount. The comparable sales of these other properties raise the value of your home because of the rehab you did on the home. With rehabbing the property you have forced the appreciation of equity to $55,000! This is on top of the monthly passive income you make each time the renter pays their rent.

New Market Value	$180,000
Purchase Price	- $100,000
Rehab Costs	- $25,000
New Equity from Forced Appreciation Through Rehab	$55,000

Analyze the Numbers and Make Sure the Property Cash Flows

This sounds like a hard thing to do, but in reality it is really only elementary school math at play here. The only caveat is if you can account for all of the expenses and income properly and anticipate future expenses that may eat into your cash flow. What it comes down to is income minus expenses equals a positive or negative cash flow. If the property rents for $1000 per month and your expenses are $1200 per month, you will lose $200 each month just by owning the property because of negative cash flow. Now if your property rents for $1000 a month and your expenses are only $750 per month, you make $250 per month positive cash flow.

There are many expenses that you will come across. Here is a list of a few you will encounter: accounting, advertising, reserve funds, electricity, insurance, management fees, pest control, repairs, poverty taxes, security services, lawn care, utilities, and other miscellaneous items. It is important to make sure that you find all the expenses for the property itemized out so you can analyze the deal accurately and not buy a bad property. You can find my Investment Property

Calculator on my website which will do all the analysis of any deal for you.

http://www.masterpassiveincome.com/
resources/investment-property-calculators/

You also want to make sure that you understand what it's going to cost to fix up the property in order to get rented. You may want to bring in a few different contractors and get multiple bids for the repairs. It is wise to know what it's going to cost to fix up the property before you buy it. Trained professionals like contractors know what to look for that a new investor would not know about.

Contact the Owner and Negotiate an Agreement with Them

This can be one of the more scary parts of the transaction process. It's always hard to approach someone you don't know and ask them if they would be willing to sell you their property for less than market value. But the more you do the easier it will get. This is the part where your personality must come out and show them that you are a credible and honest person that is willing to help them in any way possible. If they are willing to sell, you need to agree on a few things and have them put into a contract. These include purchase price, inspection period, escrow length, concessions, and/or contingencies, and other items that you discuss and agree to. The owner may be willing to carry a note on the property and basically be the banker and you pay them the mortgage each month. There are many other questions and items in the contract you need to discuss. That is in our more advanced course.

Create the Contract on the Agreed Upon Terms and the Contract with the Seller

Once you negotiated with the seller all the terms of the contract, you then need to write it up and have them sign it ASAP. By doing this, you are locking up the property so no one else can buy it from underneath you. There are many different types of templates for contracts for buying and selling a property. I used a template I got off the Internet for the first property that I bought. It worked out just fine, and those contracts are easy to find. Check our resources page for sample contracts for you to use.

www.masterpassiveincome.com/resources

Open Escrow with a Title Company

Now it's time to get a third-party involved in the deal. A third-party is somebody that's impartial to the deal and has experience in the escrow process. There are many title companies that do this, and it's up to you to find one that you are the seller both can agree upon. Escrow basically is where the title company receives your contract that is signed by both parties and holds both parties to said contract. The title company will then do a search for any liens or encumbrances against the property, making sure that the property does not have any obligations like an outstanding mortgage or overdue taxes. If the title company signs off on the property, they issue you title insurance to cover any issues they may have missed while doing the search. This insurance is there to protect you in case the title company does not do the job right.

Satisfactory Inspections

Now that escrow is open it is time for you to start your inspections of the property to make sure that you're buying a sound property. Inspections that you will probably want to have done are: home inspection, termite inspection, flood inspection, roof inspection. There are other inspections you can possibly do if you'd like, but these are the typical inspections you should do. There is an expense involved in doing these inspections, but in my opinion it's well worth it to do them. I do not want to buy a property that I will have to put tens of thousands of dollars into it because I didn't pull out of the deal when I should have.

Satisfy All Necessary Contingencies

There may be contingencies that you and the seller agree to in the negotiation process. Some contingencies may include a financing contingency, insurance contingencies, selling of a current home, appraisal, and basically anything that you and the seller agree to. You can ask for just about any type of contingency you want but it's up to the seller if they want to agree to those contingencies. It doesn't hurt to ask for a contingency if it might be necessary to have. For example, if the property is in a flood or tornado zone it might be good to have a contingency stating that the sale is contingent on you being able to get adequate insurance for the property.

Work with the Title Company to Close Escrow

Once the title work has been done and no liens are against the property and all inspections and contingencies are accounted for, it is now time to sign the escrow papers that the title company creates. Both the seller and the buyer sign the escrow papers itemizing all of the closing costs as well as the terms of the deal. That title company will then receive your money that you are required to pay the seller and distribute the proceeds of the sale to the seller. The title company will also create a deed of sale and record it with the local county recorder making the transaction public record for anyone to see. Once the deed has been recorded the property is now yours and you are ready to start rehabbing the property.

Make Ready - Rehab

Now that you have the keys to the property, it is time for you to get in there and rehab it. If you doing the work yourself you will save a lot of money, but there is a lot more work on your shoulders to get done. Doing the work yourself will also take longer than if you got a good contractor who will work on your property quickly and efficiently. A good contractor will work hard for you to get the property on the market and ready to rent as soon as possible. Be sure to account for the rehab costs when you are buying the property so you don't run out of money before you have the ability to rent it.

Find a Renter

It is now time to put the property on the markets for rent. There are many different ways to find renters, and depending on your market there are different ways for finding tenants. In some markets craigslist.com is the perfect way to find renters, and in other markets it is better to hire a realtor who matches a tenant to a property because that is the way the tenants find places to rent. Be sure to look at the market and take into account the proper amount of marketing budget you need for the property.

I always have my property managers find the tenants, show the property to them, sift through all the applications, and present the best options to me. I then have the final say, and I run a background and criminal check on all tenants that I choose to have live in my property. In the past, I was cheap and tried to save $30 per tenant by not running the background, criminal, and eviction check. I eventually realized that by running these checks on prospective tenants, I am able to weed out tenants that would possibly move out of my property quickly. It is expensive to evict a tenant. Here are some costs you may incur: eviction fees, attorney fees, writ fees, and cleaning up the property. Don't forget the loss of rents for that time that the property is not rented. I found that by spending $30 on a background check it saves me from many evictions that cost upwards of $1,000 to $1,500 in total costs.

I was so glad that I did a background, criminal, and eviction check on one lady who had been evicted four times in the last three years. That's $30 possibly saved me $1,500 in carrying costs, loss of rents, eviction fees, etc. I strongly encourage you to always run a background, criminal, and eviction check on all possible tenants. Go to http://www.masterpassiveincome.com/resources/ to find good places to do background checks.

Sign the Lease Agreement with the Tenant

This is another item that I let my property manager take care of. He meets with the tenant, has them sign the lease, and pay the first month's rent and the security deposit. Once he has all this done,he gives the tenant the keys on the designated date of the move-in. If they move-in in the middle of the month you pro-rate the rent for each day they lived there to the next month. So if they move in on June 15, there are 15 more days in the month for them to pay rent for.

If they are paying $700 a month for the rent, you divide the monthly rent($700) by the days in the month (30) days which gives you $23.33 per day. The daily rate times the amount of days the tenant will live there equals that month rent. So 15 days times $23.33 equals $350 to move in with 15 days left in the month. Many times you will get tenants that are leaving their previous place they were living in on the thirty-first and move into yours on the first of the month.

Make a Positive Return on Your Money

If you followed these steps and bought the property right you will be making a monthly return on your investment. This is from the passive income from the rent received minus the expenses for the property. Remember that the monthly rents are only one part of five different ways that you can make money.

Taking Action for Phase 3.2:

Your action items for today are:

☐ *Go to the www.masterpassiveincome. com/resources/ website and download the free sample contract to review. Read it over and be ready to fill it out on your first offer to purchase a house.*

☐ *Continue looking for properties on www. Zillow.com and keep records in the Excel spreadsheet you created a couple of days ago of the properties that interest you.*

You have just completed Phase 3.2 and are picking up steam in your investing career. Don't slack off! Get your action items done for each section.

PHASE 4 –FINISHING TOUCHES

PHASE 4.1: BUILD YOUR REAL ESTATE BUSINESS DREAM TEAM

Today is where the rubber meets the road. Now is the time where you are going to start building your business. You need to put in the leg work to build your team that is going to help you be successful in real estate. Today, you have a lot of work to do building your real estate dream team but it will all pay off in the end.

"Teamwork is the ability to work together toward a common vision. The ability to direct individual accomplishments toward organizational objectives. It is the fuel that allows common people to attain uncommon results." – Andrew Carnegie

Like all other team sports, you are only as good as the team around you. Real estate investing takes a team of people to do it well. I think of myself as a coach that has multiple players on my team, and I am the one keeping them focused on the vision that I have given them. I also give them the resources and responsibility to do what they are best at and get out of their way. Being a coach, I am not the one doing the work, my team is. They are the ones who find properties, inspect them, rehab them, get them rented, manage them, and make sure the goals are being reached.

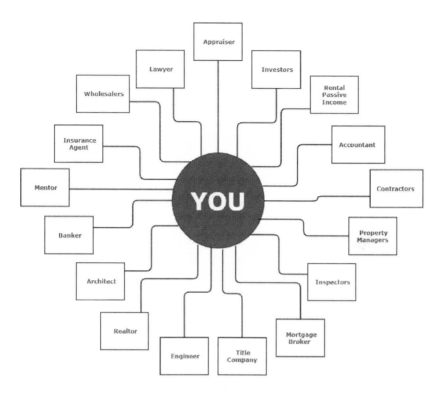

There are many different types of team members you need when you first start out investing in real estate. I suggest getting to work networking and finding the right team members for your team. If the team member doesn't fit into your team, move on and find someone else. Here is the list of team member you should have on your team:

MUST HAVE TEAM MEMBERS

1. Property Managers (PM) – If you decide to manage your properties yourself, you don't need to have a PM because you manage the property. I personally do not like to manage my own

properties so I hire a PM. If you do decide to have a PM, you must take your time and find one that you feel comfortable with and can trust.

2. **Realtors** – Realtors can be your best way to find good investment properties that bring in passive income in monthly cash flow. You should find realtors that understand how investment properties work and not just how to sell an owner occupied property. When I go into a new city to find investment properties, I usually meet with at least five different realtors and basically interview them to see if they know how to find and make offers on investment properties. If the realtor is explaining to me about how nice the window coverings are and not how much money it would take to get the property rented, I usually move on to the next realtor.

3. **Contractors** – When you find a property you want to buy and hold as a rental there usually is rehab that needs to go into the property. Everything from painting and flooring to reroofing and foundation work can be assessed by the contractor to get a quote for the repairs. This quote is important because your offer to purchase the house depends on how much money you need to put into the property to get it rented. If you need to put $5,000 into the property before you can rent it, your offer price should reflect that expense. Make your offer $5,000 lower than you would if it was 100% ready

to be rented. It is very important to know that you MAKE your profit when you BUY the house. You REALIZE the profit when you SELL it.

4. **Mortgage Brokers** – It is good to have two or three mortgage brokers on your team since funding is the life blood of the business. Without funding/leverage you would not be able to buy a home and rent it out unless you get owner financing, pay all cash, or get investors to put all the money into the deal. For most investment properties, 10%-20% would be adequate for the purchase of your rental home. If you buy a home for $80,000, your down payment would be anywhere from $8,000 to $16,000. If you shop around, you may be able to find a good broker who can get you into a home for only 10% as well as get around the Private Mortgage Insurance(PMI) because of the way they structure the mortgage.

5. **Insurance Agents** – Insurance agents are the members who will be protecting you in case there are any issues or problems that may arise on your property. Everything from fires, theft, liability, and any other possible issue with your property, your insurance agent is the one who's going to help you get through all of it. You need to make sure that you have a good agent who knows about rental properties and not just owner-occupied single-family homes. Remember, this is a business you have, and you need to make sure that you are covered well enough. It is also good to have

a general umbrella policy which is an overall liability policy that's going to protect you above and beyond your normal homeowners insurance in case there are any liability suits against you.

NICE TO HAVE TEAM MEMBERS

6. **Wholesalers and other buy and sell investors** – Wholesalers and other investors are in the real estate business but may not necessarily want to buy and hold the properties they put under contract. Wholesalers find properties that are usually not on the market and enter into a contract agreement with the homeowner to purchase their home. These wholesalers can assign the contract to you for a finder's fee and then they are out of the deal. The fee you pay the wholesalers depends on the deal and the particular wholesaler. The wholesalers usually understand how buy and hold investments work so they will bring you deals that are usually cash flow positive and bring you the passive income you need.

7. **Real Estate Investor Groups** – These are groups of investors just like you who can help you with your business. REIG are good to help you find new deals, find creative ways to structure deals, find other investors, and network with others and further build your team. www.nationalreia.com

8. **Mentors** – Finding a mentor can be one of you best resource to get started and continue to grow your real estate business. FFind a mentor that is currently where you want to be and is willing to give you an hour or two of their time monthly. It is always helpful to have someone that you can reach out to when you get stuck on a deal and you need a little helpful advice on how to get past a roadblock that is stopping you.

Mentors have the experience, the knowledge, contacts, and the willingness to help you in your investing career. It is crucial that you don't just focus on yourself when you are looking for a mentor. Having a mentor is a two-way street and the mentor must be able to get something from you in return. It would not be wise to go to a potential mentor and ask him or her to give time effort knowledge wisdom into you without offering something in return. Be sure to think of how you can benefit the mentor as you are looking to get him up on your team. You are selling yourself to them as a worthwhile investment in their time and experiences.

9. **Investors** – Like mortgage brokers, investors are the part of your team that will help you acquire the deal with as little money out of your pocket as possible. For example, you can structure a deal on a 24 unit apartment building you find with a lead

investor and passive investors. The lead investor is the one who manages the business and does all the work. Passive investors are there to help contribute their personal funds to the down payment or cash purchase of the deal. Being the lead investor, you would keep a percentage of the equity for doing all the work. This includes items like finding the deal, structuring the deal, starting/running the business, finding the investors, managing the PM, distributing the monthly/quarterly funds to the passive investors, dealing with accountants/taxes, and managing the managers of the property. Basically, the lead investor does all the work and the passive investors get a monthly/quarterly check in the mail.

10. **Title Company** – Your title company is the one that's going to make sure that the property you are buying does not have any problems. The problems could be liens against the property, back taxes, improper recording of deeds, or a host of other problems that could potentially rise. They will give you title insurance that protects you from anything they may have missed in the search for any issues with the title.

11. **Appraiser** – The appraiser is the one that is going to set a value on your property when you need it. You cannot always use your own appraiser but it is always good to have someone on your team that

can give you some advice on the value of your property.

12. **Lawyers** – It is said that in real estate, it's not IF you get sued, it's only a matter of WHEN. It is wise to have a lawyer on your team, not necessarily one that you pay and have as a retainer, but someone that you are able to call when something goes wrong. Be sure it is the type of lawyer that handles real estate and/or rental property issues.

13. **Banker** – Your banker is someone that will help you get loans that you would probably not normally get. Bankers don't just look at your credit score and financial history, they also look at you and see if you are the type of person they want to do business with and someone who can pay off the loan. If you work with a banker and you are not presentable in a professional way the banker may not feel that you are able to pay off the loan. Even though the property will bring in money enough to pay for the mortgage and provide you income the banker may think that you would not pay the mortgage but just keep all the money for yourself. Be sure to get a banker on your team.

Whenever I go into a new area to invest, I always work on my team before I even start. In each area where I invest, I have a different team. Some, like mortgage brokers, can be used all over the state or country and be on multiple teams at the same time. Others, like realtors and PM's, can only be local because you need the people on the ground in each market where you invest. They are your eyes and ears for your business, and they keep the business running with you out of the picture.

Find the best players to be on your team. This is a marathon, not a sprint. Get the players that will last the long haul and help your team win at the end of the race.

WHAT TO LOOK FOR IN A PROPERTY MANAGER

Your real estate business depends on who you have managing the property and how they manage it as well. If you manage the properties yourself, great, more power to you. I personally do not want to manage my own properties, so I hire a Property Manager (PM) to manage it for me. I would rather spend my time on the things that I want and pay my PM to manage the property for me. I love receiving my rent checks each month from my property manager and not having to do a thing to get it. All my work was done in the beginning when I bought the property and set up my business. Now it is on autopilot.

Here is a good start to finding the right property manager for your real estate business. Since I invest all over the country, I depend on my PM's doing the job right and the way I expect them to. When I am looking for a new property manager, I always meet with a 4-5 property managers in person while they show me the area I am going to start investing. I like to meet with at least four different PM's so I hopefully find one, and a backup, that will take care of my business well. The items in the list below are non-negotiable for me when I look for a property manager. There are other things I look for in a PM but I will not do without these. The only way to find out if your property manager has these qualities is to build a relationship with him and ask many questions.

HERE ARE THE SIX DEAL BREAKERS FOR PROPERTY MANAGERS

Trustworthiness

You must be able to trust your PM. Remember, they are your employee, and they are working for you. One property manager I had was not trustworthy, and I had to fire her. There were missing receipts, unexplained expenses, upset tenants, etc. Don't put up with a bad property manager. Get rid of them quickly. Like any employee you have, hire slow, fire fast.

Don't put up with a bad property manager. Get rid of them quickly. I treat them like any employee I have ever employed. If they are good, I treat and pay them well. They are running my business for me, and if it was not for them, I would not have a business. But if they are a bad employee I get rid of them as fast as possible.

Accountability

Everything the PM does should be run through you, and you should be able to verify what they do. I give my PM's the authority to spend under $100 per property per month without my approval. I don't want to be bothered with a $5 toilet leak, but I do want to be bothered about a $300 water heater or a $2,000 furnace replacement.

I review every statement and every expense/income that I receive. If there are any issues or questions, I ask them right away. If the PM is unable to adequately answer my questions, I start to get suspicious of them doing their job well and how much I can trust them. Once the seed of doubt is planted, it takes a lot of time for the PM to build that trust back up in me so I am able to fully trust them.

Communication

The PM should be able to return your call/text/email within the same day, or at the latest, within 24 hours. This is a non-negotiable. Only with good communication can your real estate business run well and keep you and your tenants happy. I have had bad PM's in the past and they make your life too hard to keep them. I find that the main problem with a lack of communication is that I start to worry about my properties and imagine the worst possible scenarios for my properties. I employ my PM so that I don't have to think about the property and if he/she is not communicating promptly; my properties are all that I think about.

When I am screening out PM's before I invest in a new area I expect the PM to be on their "A" game and be in constant conversation with me because he wants to get my business. If the PM has horrible communication timelines and abilities while he is trying to get my business, I can only imagine how much worse it would be when I actually hire him to do the job. I have passed on many PM's because of their lack of communication in the hiring period because it will more than likely get worse, not better.

Quality of Work

When you have a good PM, the quality of the rehab or repairs she will do should meet your standards. You should be able to rely on your PM to make the property desirable to tenants and get top dollar for the rent. If your properties are run down, the rent amount will be much lower than if you take care of the properties because they are not as desirable. Your PM is who makes sure the property is desirable. If you are not able to get the same market rents as the properties near you, look into the quality of product your PM is selling to the prospective tenants.

References

Just like hiring any other employee, check their references, and see if they have a good track record with previous/current landlords they are working for. If they have good references you have hopefully been able to get a leg up on finding a good PM.

I never understood when PM's do not give references. I had one potential PM tell me that he will not give any references because his other landlords are confidential. This was a huge red flag for me. No matter the reason for him being secretive, this goes against points two and three. It shows that they do not want to be held accountable and that they may not be trustworthy enough for me to hire them. I moved on.

Commission Percentage

The amount that I pay my PM is based on what I contract with them for their services. Some areas 8% of rents is the going rate and in others 10% is. If it is hard to find a good PM in a specific area, you may pay an awesome PM 12% because you are getting awesome service for your money. I have an area where I am paying 12% for my PM, but he is worth every penny.

The biggest thing I can leave you with is this: When you get a good PM, pay them and treat them well. The PM whom I pay 12% of the rents, which is rather high for a percentage, is worth every penny. One day I thought to change the terms of our agreement once and bring the % down to 10%. After I considered the change, the amount of money I would save would not compare to the amount of dissatisfaction my PM would feel. The decrease would lower his desire to do the job right. Just imagine if your boss came to you and asked you to take a pay decrease all while you are the one making the money for him. That wouldn't be good at all.

Again, when you find a good property manager, pay them what they deserve.

QUESTIONS TO ASK PROPERTY MANAGERS

Property managers are absolutely vital in this line of business. If you do not have a good property manager, your business will go down the drain, and you will lose money and possibly lose your properties. I have experience in property managers that have lied, stole money, put false expenses on my properties, and all of this could've been avoided by finding a good property manager. Below is a list of questions that I asked prospective property managers when I'm going to start investing in a new area. What you want to find is a property manager that you can trust and can give the responsibility of running your business.

This initial phone conversation is just the start of a long relationship with your property manager. Your goal here is to get information as well as start developing a report with the property manager. You want to find somebody that you can get along with and enjoy working with them. I learned a long time ago that I do not want to work with anyone whom I do not like to be around. Life is too short to waste it on people that make your life harder and take lots of energy to deal with.

Here are some questions I ask potential property managers:

■ How long have you been a property manager?

This question is more of a general question for your information. I have had bad property managers that have had many years of experience. I've also had good property managers that had no experience. I would suggest finding a property manager that has experience managing properties if you are new to rental properties. Remember that property managers are your employee, and they need to follow your business rules. If they do not follow your instructions and it seems like they are possibly lying to you, it may be time to get rid of them. Like hiring any employee, you want to hire slow and fire fast. Make sure you hire the right person the first time because it takes a lot of work to fire them. After you fire a PM, you need to spend the time to find somebody new, train him, and start your business building again.

■ How many properties are you managing right now?

This too is another question that is more for your information and is not necessarily a deal breaker. Obviously, the more properties the property manager is managing tends to normally be a good sign but not necessarily. It is just a number that they are telling you and would be hard to verify. I just like to have a conversation with them to see if I hit it off with them and I feel comfortable working with them.

■ How many vacancies do you have right now?

The percentage of vacancy units for a property owner should be as low as possible. To find the vacancy rate, you divide the number of vacant months by the total months of the year. If a tenant stays in the property for one year, that would be a 0% vacancy factor. If a single family home is vacant for one month, then the vacancy rate would be 8% (1 month / 12 months = 8%).

The vacancy rate right now is a good indication of the market and the property manager as well. The market might be a rough area to rent properties, meaning that the tenants move in and out quickly and there is high turnover. I have rented in some areas that I would probably have one eviction per year if I'm not really on top of everything. Places like this, it seems like the tenants change homes like they change their shirts. I personally don't see how they can do that. I hate moving.

The vacancy rate also shows how well the property manager keeps his properties rented. If he does not do a good job with maintaining the properties, keeping the tenants content, and knowing what amount of rent to charge for a particular home, vacancies will get high. Remember that you are in the service business when you're renting properties. If the service you're providing, which is a home for a renter, is not up to market standards, you are going to lose tenants quickly and lose money.

■ **How long does it take, on average, to fill a vacancy?**

This is a great question because the longer property is not rented the more money you lose. If your property rents for $700 a month and the property is vacant for 1 ½ months that's $1050 out of your pocket in lost revenue because the property is vacant.

Did you create your own lease and property manager contracts? If no, where did you get them? Please send them to me so I can review them.

I like to look at the lease my property managers are going to use because it shows me what type of manager they are and what they expect from other tenants. If the lease is very lenient, the property manager may be lenient on the tenant and possibly allow problems to arise and may cost you money in the long run. If the contract is very strict and rigid you protect yourself from many unforeseen issues and are covered when something goes wrong. You want a property manager that will take care of your property and keep the tenants accountable to do the same. Just know that a strict property manager may be pretty meticulous and on top of things which will help make and save you money.

■ What is your late rent policy?

Some property managers charge $40, $50, $75 for late charge from the tenants. Depending on the area and tenants, I usually leave this is up to the property manager to decide. I have had some property managers that do keep the late fees for themselves, and I've also had others that split the late fee with me 50-50. The property manager needs to keep at least 50% of the money because they are the ones doing the work with collecting on late rents which can be a headache.

■ What percentage of tenants do you have to evict?

Some areas may have a very low eviction rate, and others may be very high. I have found that the lower class markets tend to have more evictions than the middle to upper class markets. For whatever reason it is, I've just seen that to be true. In the places where you have high eviction rates, the key is to do a thorough background check on the prospective tenant. Make sure you do a criminal, credit, and eviction check on the tenant before they move-in.

■ Would you please explain to me the eviction process in your area?

Each city, county, and state all have different laws for the eviction process, and it is wise to learn the process as you are getting started with buying rental properties. Your property manager should know the eviction process and also what to do and not do while he is evicting the tenant. You don't want to break any laws, but you do want to get the bad tenants out quickly so you can get good ones in.

■ What are your management fees?

Management fees vary from area to area and even manager to manager. An average fee would be 8% to 10% of the total rents collected each month. You may get some higher some lower, but remember you get what you pay for. I have one area where I pay 12% to my property manager, but he is worth every single penny.

■ What do you charge for finding new tenants?

This is basically a finders fee for finding new tenants for your property. The manager has to do marketing, showing the property, taking applications, signing leases, preceding the first month rent and security deposit, and giving the tenant the keys to move in. This is a lot of work, and your property manager should be paid for it. Some charge the entire first month's rent as a finders fee, but I personally find that to be ridiculous.

If your PM does charge a high finders fee make sure it is in writing that you will only pay that fee one time each year from the date it is rented. This is to protect you so that you don't have to pay again if you have to find a new tenant in the same year. The property manager's job is to find a good tenant, one that will stay there for many years, and not just turnover in six months. One area that I am in I pay my property manager $100 finders fee every time the properties rented even if it is in the same year which I have had in the past.

■ **If a property is vacant, do you charge for monitoring and maintaining vacant units?**

This type of fee is a huge red flag for me. If the property is not rented, I am not making money. And in turn the property manager should not be making money because he is responsible getting the property rented and for keeping it rented. If I am not getting paid, then my property managers not getting paid.

Doesn't it seem like a conflict of interest if the property manager charges $50 if the property is not rented, but also makes $60 if the property is rented? There is only a $10 incentive for him to get the property rented, which is not very much. I stay away from property managers who charge this. But even if they do, I have negotiated some out of this charge because I will not pay it and they remove it.

■ **Do you also market properties as a broker?**

This is an interesting question because, like I said, in some areas the marketing can be craigslist.com or may even be through the MLS and need a broker to rent them out. Either way, it doesn't really matter, in my opinion. I just like to know.

■ **If I decide to sell my property, do I have to list it with you?**

Some PMs may require this in the contract that they sign with you. I would completely strike it out and remove that from the contract or find new property manager.

■ **Can I see some of the other properties you manage?**

If you're in the area and can see the properties, it's always a good idea to look at how the property manager does his business. I also like to talk to the tenants to ask them questions like; How do you like the property? How long have you lived here? How long does it take for the property manager to return your phone calls? How long does it take for him to respond to repairs needed?

■ **Do you recommend special incentives for tenants?**

In some cases, it may be good to offer incentives to prospective tenants or even current tenants. I invest in one area that snows heavily and gets very cold. So if I have a vacant property in November I dropped the rent amount $75-$100 to get it rented before it starts to freeze.

I have some tenants that have lived in my properties for over three to four years, and I like to give them a little something to show them my appreciation for being such great tenants. They can be a small gift card to Home Depot or Lowe's or even Starbucks. I also like to have a thank you card for them expressing my gratitude. A little gratitude goes a long way.

■ **If I want additional marketing for specific vacant units, how would we arrange that?**

If there is a property that has been vacant too long, or one that I don't want to stay vacant long at all, I may want the property manager to go above and beyond his normal marketing for this property.

■ **How do you screen prospects?**

There many ways to screen prospects for your properties, and your property manager should do all of them for you. This includes things like checking employment history, checking rental history, checking references, and even running a background, credit, criminal, and eviction checks.

It is also helpful if your property manager is able to accurately judge the character of potential renters quickly. Some people have a gift of discernment that helps in this process, and some do not. It is just wise to listen to your property manager to see if they like the tenant or not and if they desire to rent to them.

■ **Do you give each applicant a credit, criminal, and eviction check?**

Doing a credit, criminal, and eviction check is an absolute must for me and my properties. I have been burned so many times because of not doing these checks and have fully implemented them into my business. A $30 background check will save me at least a thousand dollars a year in eviction fees and lost rents. If the property manager will not do it, make sure that you will have the ability to do one yourself.

■ **How do you collect rent, and when is the rent due?**

In some areas, a personal check is just fine, and in other areas cash or cashier's check is the only way to do business. Depending on the area, you need to do what you can to make sure that you get your rent on time, every time, without any issues.

The rent is always due on the first of the month and is late on the second. On the second, if they do not pay the rent, you give them a three day notice letting them know that the eviction will start on the fifth of the month. Once you start the eviction process, don't stop until you get every penny back from the eviction process. I make the tenant pay all the fees I incur, late fees, and the rent due.

■ **How do your tenants contact you?**

This is more for your information, and it probably varies by property manager and even tenant. It's always good to have a property manager that can have multiple ways of contact; email, text, phone, and even mail.

■ **What is your maximum response time?**

For tenants, I think an adequate maximum response time from the property manager is 24 hours. Anything longer than 24 hours, you are going to start losing money. Your tenants are your customer, which means they are the property managers' customers. You must make sure they are well taken care of.

■ **If I am unable to reach you, what is your maximum response time to get back to me?**

For me, the maximum response time should be 12 hours after I contact my property manager. If my property manager does not respond to me within 12 hours I start to get concerned about my properties and my property manager. There should be no reason for a property manager to take more than 12, or possibly even 24 hours, to get back to you. Anything longer than that is just unacceptable. Communication is huge in this business. I live as far as 1500 miles away from a place where I invest so I rely on communication.

Taking Action for Phase 4.1:

Your action items for today are:

☐ *Start building your real estate dream team by searching the Internet for the "Must Have" team members. Make a list of at least five different possible team members for each type of "Must Have" member.*

☐ *Get on the phone and call as many property managers as you can find. You are basically interviewing the PM's because you are hiring them to run your business. Try to select three to five managers that you think may make a good team member. Eventually, you will select one or possibly two PM's that you will work with on your team.*

You have just completed Phase 4.1 of the How to Quit Your Job with Rental Properties eBook and are almost finished! Remember, it is crucial that you complete the action items each day and not let things slip by.

PHASE 4.2: FIND, EVALUATE, VALUE, AND BUY A PROPERTY

I n this Phase, we will be learning all about how to find properties, evaluate properties, and evaluate the numbers to make sure the deal makes you money. Now the fun work begins, and pretty soon you'll start having passive income through your rental properties. Let's do this!

HOW TO FIND PROPERTIES

We have learned a little about how to find properties earlier in the week, but this is going to be where you learn many different tricks of the trade and how to find a good deal on a rental property. Let's just dive right in.

Business Cards and Flyers

> I buy houses, duplexes, multi-unit apartments, and commercial.
> I will look at all in any condition.
>
> **Dustin Heiner**
> 555-4321

If you are going to be a serious investor, print out business cards and flyers. The printing of the business cards is not expensive and is an affordable way to enhance your image and get your message out that you are a real estate investor. You can put on the card something that catches people attention like: "**I buy houses, duplexes, multi unit apartments, and commercial buildings. I will look at all, in any condition.**" Give these business cards out to anyone and everyone that you talk to about your business. If people don't know that you do real estate, how are they going to help you find a new property or even sell you the one that they currently own? So use these business cards and give them out freely.

The flyers that you print up can be made very cheaply, and you can even print them from your home computer. As you are driving neighborhoods looking for a property to buy, you may come across one that looks neglected. The lawn has weeds in it that are growing as tall as your knees, cobwebs all over the house, paint is peeling, and other signs that the house is in disrepair. These flyers can be put on the doorstep or even in the mailbox if it's possible. You never know when a deal will present itself.

Direct Mail

Direct mail is when you go out and bring sellers to you by using an address list of all the properties that you would like to pursue and directly sending them a letter inquiring if they want to sell their house. There are many different ways to do this, but a good template to use is called the "yellow letter" direct mail campaign. It is as simple as it sounds.

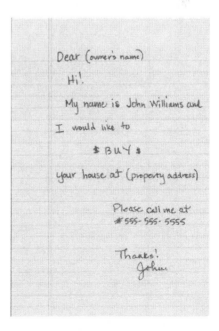

You get a yellow notepad and handwrite a letter to the owners of the property asking them if they are willing to sell their property.

Classified Ads

Even though newspapers are starting to be out of date, a lot of people still read them and go to them for classified ads. Some of the best leads on properties can come from for sale by owner (FSBO) ads. These ads can show the motivation of the seller and can give you a little insight into why they are selling and give you the opportunity to help them with their problem they're having with their home. Maybe they are moving out of town because of their job or they need to sell because they bought a new house. In any case, it gives you a place to start negotiating from. In classified ads you want to look for ads that say something of the following: handyman special, distress sale, divorce must sell, owner transferred, must sell!

www.craigslist.com

Another great place is craigslist.com. This is the online version of the classified ad. Many people are using it today and will in the future. It is so simple to use and free! You can even use craigslist to find a specific type of the house, like a three bedroom two bathroom home listed for $100,000. You will see homes that are for sale by owner and ones that are listed by a real estate agent. Never overlook an opportunity that you find by running the numbers. Over time, you will begin to have the ability to look at a property online and in two minutes determine if it is worth your time to move forward with evaluating the property further.

www.zillow.com

As we talked about earlier in the week, Zillow is a good website to find properties that are listed or are possibly for sale by owner. It also gives you the ability to see their estimated value of the property and their estimated rent amount. This site takes all the comparable sales of the property in the general area and finds the value, as well as looks for other homes that are currently for rent in the area and gives you the average rent for that type of property. I would not go with these numbers to manage my deal, but I use them as a quick head start before I spend my time doing all my own work valuing the property.

Legal Notices

In the classified section of most newspapers, there is an area for legal notices. Under this section you will find IRS seized properties and properties that are being foreclosed upon. Usually, the attorney handling the case will have his name or his firm's name somewhere in the posting. You can call them directly and find out more about the property so you can figure out if this is a good property to buy.

You can also buy properties that have delinquent property taxes on the courthouse steps. Different counties have different rules about buying these tax delinquent properties, and there are many books written on this type of buying of property. Buying property from the courthouse steps is not easy and does have many hurdles and pitfalls that you must know how to navigate. A big one is that you must provide the full purchase price within 24 hours of the closing auction. Another huge issue is that more than likely you are not able to see the property before you buy it. So, you are gambling on the deal because you don't always know the numbers and will not know how much money it's going to take to get the property ready for rent.

Drive-Bys

This is where you get in your car and drive the neighborhoods that you are interested in pursuing. You want to look for distressed properties and any others that catch your eye. Write down the address of the property for future research. You can also leave the flyers that you created or your business card on the door for the owner to see. Keep your eyes open while you're driving anywhere. You may see a property that you want to pursue on your way to dinner with your spouse. Keep a running list of all the property addresses for your research.

In most counties all over the nation, the county assessor or tax collector has the ownership information for all of the properties in the county. When you go to the assessor or tax collector, look up the owner either on the tax rolls or by the assessor parcel number of the property. You will find that the workers in the county office building will be quite helpful in locating the name and address of the owner. Sometimes the owner doesn't live on the property, so there is a mailing address that you need to get, not just the physical address of the property. Then you can write or call the owner to ask him if he is interested in selling. This is not the best way to find a good property as a deal, but it is a tool to have in your tool belt to find properties.

So as you are driving, keep a list of all the addresses that you are interested in pursuing. Once you have a good list of all properties, you go to the county department that has the ownership information, and look up the owner's names and addresses. A lot of counties are now putting all their information online, so be sure to check the county website to see if they offer ownership information online. You can even give the county office a call before you do anything and asked them the process of finding out ownership information.

Real Estate Agents

Real estate agents are on the front lines of the real estate market and can find you good deals. There are a few things to keep in mind when you're looking for real estate agents. The biggest thing is to find an agent who is familiar with investing in rental properties and not just looking for a house for a homeowner to live in. I've had some realtors show me homes who treated me like I was going be living in the property, which is not necessarily bad, just not what I was looking for. That gave me an indication that this person doesn't understand that I'm an investor who is looking for good deals for rental properties. You want to find a realtor that specializes in investment properties.

I have had some real estate agents want me to sign an exclusive deal with them. This is where any property I buy must go through them as my agent even if I find the property myself. I just laugh at this type of realtor. These realtors just want to make money and don't really want to help you. So if I find a property on my own, I am required by my contract to buy through this realtor because she has an exclusive right to all my transactions in real estate. These exclusive contracts are ridiculous and only benefit the realtor. I will never sign an exclusive deal with anyone because that limits what I can do on my own or with other realtors.

What I do is create a team of realtors that find properties, and whoever brings me the property gets the deal. The other realtors don't necessarily work together, but they are all working for me, finding me properties. They are working while I am doing whatever I want. I do believe that if someone brings you the deal they should be the ones to close on it and not somebody else.

A great benefit of a realtor is they can set you up with an MLS Internet-based search that will alert you when properties that fit your criteria come on the market. They can create an account for you in their system that allows you to login and look at all the properties that are currently listed for sale. This is a very handy tool because it keeps all of your potential properties together in one place for you to review. Just talk to a realtor about setting you up with one of these accounts, and they will be more than happy to do so.

Wholesalers

Wholesalers are investors who find good deals on properties and sell them to other investors while taking a commission for finding the property. The commission usually ranges from $4,000-$6,000 and all depends on what you negotiate with them. They are really good to have on your team because they are doing all the hard work for you finding good deals on properties. They do all the things we just talked about: getting business cards, going to classified ads, going to the newspaper, check the Internet, go through all the legal notices, tax information, do drive-bys, and talk to people one-on-one.

It's very easy to find wholesalers. Keep your eye out the next time you're driving around a neighborhood for signs that are nailed to a telephone pole that reads "I buy houses for cash fast!" or something like that. These are called bandit signs and are a crude but effective way to find deals for wholesalers. People see these everywhere, and if they are considering selling they will call the number on the sign and talk to the wholesaler directly about selling the property to them. In any city, you will find these all over, so just keep your eyes peeled for them.

HOW TO EVALUATE THE PROPERTY AND ANALYZE THE DEAL

A big concern that most people have when they start investing in real estate is, "What do I do when there are problems?" You need to remember that this is a business, and there is a cost of doing business in any type of business you own. The goal is to have the income be more than the expenses every month which brings in a positive passive income. When the expenses are more than your income, you have a negative cash flow every month, and that is not what you want. If you buy right, you can make positive cash flow each month from the business rather than having to put money into the business. I have owned other types of businesses, like a retail store that took money out of my pocket because of the bad economy in 2009. The store I owned was doing well until the recession hit, and then it started taking money out of my pocket. Even through the recession my rental properties kept making me money even though my business was losing me money.

Like any business you need to plan how to do business properly. You need to value the property right by including all possible expense like: property taxes, vacancy allowance, maintenance expense, capital improvements, and other foreseeable expenses, and account for these in your valuation. If the deal does not make money in cash flow every month when you buy it, it is not a property to buy. Master passive income is about making money each month in cash flow from the rents of the property. Even though there are numerous other ways to benefit from a rental property, cash flow is what is going to help you quit your job because you have income coming in whether you work or not.

When you evaluate the property, you should always get a home inspection from a certified inspector on every home I purchase. They are trained, experienced, and paid to find problems with a property. I never want to be caught off guard when issues arise. I am proactive and want to see things coming because I have many options. If I become reactionary, my options are limited and more than likely will cost me more money.

Evaluating the Property

What often scares most newcomers in the investing in real estate world is that a property takes too much money to fix up to get rented and to make it a good investment. In all my investing I rarely have ever seen a property that is too far gone to not negotiate with the owner over. Just about all property can be repaired. It only matters how much it cost to do so. These properties can still be good investments because if the property is in really bad shape, the owner may be motivated to sell much lower than the market value of a similar property that is in good condition. Depending on the price you negotiate with the seller, these "bad" properties can be a great deal for you.

If you find a home is worth $150,000 in great condition, and it is only worth $80,000 because of its dilapidated condition, it may possibly still be a good deal for you because of the value you can bring. By fixing up, rehabbing, and repairing the property you can make it worth the $150,000 that it should be worth. This is possible because when you put in an offer to the seller you need to itemize out all the repairs needed for the property so the seller can see that the home is not worth market value but much less because of all the repairs. If there are $60,000 in repairs needed for the property, that may be very daunting for the seller to try to do himself, but you, as an investor, put that in your numbers.

This property that you found that can be worth $150,000 but needs $60,000 in repairs would require an offer of $50,000 to the seller because of all the work needed to repair the property. When you present the offer, walk the owner through each repair needed and the costs involved that add up to your $60,000 in repairs. Show the owner that the property will need a lot of work in order to be livable and/or sellable. Remember that a house is a product, and a product is only worth what other people are willing to buy it for. If the owner does not want to sell it for $50,000, then it's not a good deal, and it's time for you to walk away. Never get emotionally attached to any deal because you may make a bad business decision and buy a house that loses you money. There are many other homes out there for you to invest in.

Some things to consider when you evaluate a property

Structural Damage

If the foundation is bad or the property is leaning in one direction, you need to get a few contractors to look at the property and give you an estimate of the repair costs. Always get multiple quotes when you are doing repairs on a property. You will have to look at your numbers and see if you can make the deal still work with the repair costs by adjusting your offer price. In the interior, you may have some foundation issues if you have floors that are dramatically pitched toward any specific direction. The foundation may be cracked or sinking, and you also need to have a contractor come and give you an estimate of the repair costs. Don't let this scare you, but you can use it to negotiate an even better price for the property because of all the work. Remember, you are getting paid for the value you bring not for the hours you work. You need to evaluate each circumstance individually and make your decision based on the rehab money that you have allocated to the project.

Termite Damage

Depending on which part of the country you live in, termites can be more problematic in some than others, and it is wise to get a termite inspection when you buy a house. If there is termite damage, don't let that scare you because it can take up to 10 or 15 years before termites can do irreparable damage. Like with structural damage, make sure you get a contractor to assess the damages and give you an estimate of the repairs needed to make the property whole again. Also, get an estimate of cost to eradicate the termites so nothing happens again. Like all expenses, make sure you put this number in your offer price so you don't overpay for a property.

Roof Damage

Always examine the roof. You should also get a roofer to look at it for you, and have them give you a roof certification. These certifications are inspections done by the roofer and guarantee the roof to not leak within two years of the inspection. If it looks like the roof will need replacing in the near future, put that into your offer as well. Set enough money aside for the repairs from your home improvement loan and let it accumulate interest until the roof starts leaking and you need to replace it.

If the first roofer will not certify the roof and tells you that it needs to be replaced, get two or three other roofers to inspect and certify the roof. If they all say that the roof needs to be replaced, then have them each give you an estimate for re-roofing the property,and go with the one you feel the strongest about. I do not always go with the lowest price estimate but also take into consideration the person doing the work.

Major Plumbing

While evaluating a property, turn on all the faucets, flush all the toilets, and make sure all the drains run freely. It is common for older buildings to have galvanized or cast-iron plumbing which can be a problem. After years of use, these pipes can collect sediment which builds up and causes a loss of water pressure and stops up drains. If you run across any issues with pressure or the draining of water, get a plumber to give you an estimate of the repairs needed.

Electrical

When you go through a house, hopefully, the electricity is currently on and you can test electrical throughout the house. Go through every room of the house and turn on the lights, check sockets, test the oven, check out the breaker box, and make sure that the electrical working properly. If you find any issues, get an electrician to assess the damages and give you an estimate for the repairs. Like all other repairs, reflect these in your offer price.

In one area that I invest, the county code states that if a property has not had electricity on for one year, then an electrical inspection must be done by the county inspectors. The code states that the inspection must be done before the electricity can be turned on. This is not usually an issue, but the properties in the area are mostly older homes that have outdated electrical throughout the entire home. As soon as a government inspector comes into your property they can shut you down quickly and easily if they decide that your property is not up to code.

On a few different houses, the inspection came up that the entire electrical throughout the house needed to be brought up to code before the electricity could be turned on. This was a $2,000 cost that I put in the offer as a repair needed to be done. If I did not account for this $2,000 in electrical repairs, that money would have come out of my pocket. As it is, I put the cost in the offer price and lowered my offer by $2,000, so basically the seller paid for the upgraded electrical.

Furnaces and HVAC Units

HVAC stands for "heating ventilation and air-conditioning." It is wise to have these inspected before you purchase a property because it is quite costly to replace them if it's needed. If in the near future these systems need to be replaced, this should reflect in the cost of your offer price. One area where I invest is in Ohio where it snows a lot and gets very cold. My tenants rely heavily on the furnaces to be functioning and work well throughout the winter. Furnaces can cost anywhere from $2,000 to $5,000 to replace depending on the size efficiency.

I have had to replace a number of furnaces and have found, like always, it is best to get multiple quotes when you are shopping for a new HVAC system. One company wanted to charge me $4,000 for a new furnace, and I found another smaller company that only charged me $1,800. The $4,000 unit would definitely be a much more efficient and higher capacity unit, but it was too big for my property, and the labor charges from the company were too high. I went with the $1,800 furnace and have not had any complaints from my tenants since.

Evaluating the Property: Conclusion

These are areas where you could have some major expenses if there is a problem. In most cases, though, the roof, plumbing, and heating units need to be replaced or have a major repair only every 20 to 25 years. So you do not need to expect these problems, but have them in mind because they are the exception and not the rule. The big thing to keep in mind is that when you see these problems think of them as moneymakers for you and don't rule out the property because of them. If you can cover the repairs and still make money on the property, the property is a good investment. And remember to put the repair costs into the offer price, and try to pay less for the property.

FIND THE VALUE OF THE DEAL

It is really not hard to find the value of the deal and if it's going to make you money or not. It is only basic arithmetic that you learned in elementary school. You just need to know the formula to put together to value the deal. So how do you figure out what the cash return will be after a year of ownership? You should calculate your return before you ever make a purchase or even make an offer. This is the only way to make an intelligent decision as to whether or not the return on your money is worth buying the property. The best way to evaluate the return to see if the property is worth buying is by analyzing the cash on cash return for the property. Basically, if you invest X amount of dollars and can't return at least 30% in the first year then you should not make the deal.

When you look at the stock market, which gives you at best at 10% return every year, anything above that should be good, right? Thirty percent return is actually a very low number, and I have even seen returns as much as 100%, 200%, and even 500%. This goal of 30% is there to help you in two ways. First of all, so you can make a good return on your money, and secondly, to protect you from any errors that you may have made when you evaluated the property, and it gives you some room to still make money.

NET PROFIT VALUATION

Step 1 - Calculate gross rents, both yearly and monthly.

Step 2 - Add up in total all variable expenses, both yearly in monthly.

Step 3 - Add up in total yearly mortgage payments.

Step 4 - Deduct variable expenses and mortgage payments from your gross rents.

Step 5 - Take your net figure and divide it by your down payment. This will give you a percentage figure that will give you a rate of return on your invested cash.

Examples: $500 / $2,000 = 25%
$4,000 / $2,000 = 200%
$5,000 / $2,000 = 250%

Five Ways to Make Money (Example):
In a single family home with a $10,000 down payment the analysis would look like this:

Rent:	Monthly	Yearly
Total:	$1,100	$13,200

Expenses:	Monthly	Yearly
Taxes:	$100	$1,200
Insurance:	$50	$600
Water and Sewer:	Tenants Pay	
Utilities:	Tenants Pay	
Advertising:	$10	$120
Vacancy 5%:	$55	$660
Total:	$215	$2,580

Mortgage Debt:	Monthly	Yearly
1st Mortgage:	$538	$6,456
2nd Mortgage:	$0	$0
Total:	$538	$6,456

	Monthly	Yearly
Gross Rents	$1,100	$13,200
- Expenses	$215	$2,580
- Mortgage Debt	$538	$6,456
NET CASH FLOW:	**$347**	**$4,164**

Since the total investment you put in the deal was the $10,000 down payment on the property, take the net yearly cash flow of $4,164, and divide it by the total investment of $10,000. **$4,164 / $10,000 = 0.4164 = 42% return on your money in the first year!** Imagine if you only put down $5,000 on the property; your return would be 83% in the first year! Try to get that in the stock market!

EQUITY CAPTURE

Remember that you make your money when you buy the property, and you realize your money when you sell it. This is what equity capture is all about. You do not want to buy a property for market rate because you do not make any money to buy the property.

Market Value:	$125,000
Purchase Price:	-$100,000
NET EQUITY CAPTURE	**$25,000**

To calculate the return on your investment (ROI) on the equity capture, you divide the equity capture amount by the total investment to get your return. **$25,000 / $10,000 = 250% ROI!**

APPRECIATION VALUATION

If you know your market, you will be able to estimate how much specific improvements will increase the value of your property. Appreciation on your property turns into cash profit when you sell or refinance the property.

Revised appraised value of property:	$155,000
Original purchase price of the property:	-$100,000

Cost of improvements:	-$8,000
FORCED APPRECIATION:	**$47,000**

To calculate the return on your investment (ROI) on the appreciation, you divide the forced appreciation amount by the total investment to get your return. $47,000 / $10,000 = 470% ROI!

EQUITY BUILDUP

As rents pay down the mortgage balance, the equity increase is considered profit. The equity is only on paper until you sell or refinance the property.

Purchase Price:	$100,000
down payment:	-$10,000
Initial loan amount:	$90,000
amount applied to principal:	-$800
new principal balance:	**$89,200**

To calculate the equity buildup ROI divide the amount of equity by the initial investment of $10,000 for the down payment. **$800 / $10,000 = 8% ROI**

TAX ADVANTAGES

With investing in real estate, you get many tax advantages because the laws are written to benefit those who own real estate. You will be able to offset most, if not all, of your income for tax purposes because of depreciation. The IRS states that your property is going down in value, and you can depreciate your property over 27 years, and that depreciation offsets your income from the property. How much of the tax advantage you get from depreciation depends on your tax bracket and your sources of income. It's generally around 5 to 15% ROI from this tax advantage on your initial investment.

RECAP OF THE EVALUATION AND ROI

Net Cash Flow	42%
Equity Capture	250%
Forced Appreciation	470%
Equity Buildup	8%
Tax Advantage (average estimate)	10%
1st YEAR TOTAL RATE OF RETURN	780%

Can you believe you could make 780% ROI on your investment in one year! Try to get that in the stock market, bonds, treasury bills, or any other investment. Hopefully, you can see that you can make tremendous amounts of money in rental properties, and all it takes is the knowledge to do so and the drive to put into action. These numbers can get a little confusing, but I encourage you to look this section over again on how rental properties can make you money five different ways.

HOW TO FINANCE YOUR PROPERTIES

One of the major questions most people ask is: "How do you finance your properties?" There are many different ways to finance your deals, and yes, there are ways to buy rentals with no money down. Even though you see many late-night infomercials with some guru telling you that anyone can buy real estate with no money down, it is very hard to do. I have found that it usually does take money to make money. The way I suggest to buy and hold onto real estate is through the "7 Cures for a Lean Purse" from the book The Richest Man In Babylon. One of the cures for a lean purse is all about paying yourself first. This means to take 10% of your income each month and save it for future investments. When you have saved enough money for a down payment on a rental property, you can then buy a rental and then start over again. The beauty part is the more properties you get, the easier it is to buy more because of the increased income from the rents received each month. Getting rich in real estate does not happen overnight and does take some intentional hard work.

You are a real estate investor, and it is your job to find creative tactics to finance your deals. You can use one type of financing or combine multiple together to get the deal done. As we are going through these different types of financing, try not to get overwhelmed because there is a lot to learn. You do not have to learn all of them at the same time, but it is good to know of what types are possible for you. Each deal that you find for a property has unique circumstances that may require you to get creative by using one or two of these financing tactics. You should focus on a couple of these tactics I outline below, and try to learn as much as you can about each one. Try to keep your mind open, though, to the other tactics for financing your properties so that when you hit a roadblock on a financing deal, you can do more research on how to use the other tactics to finance the deal.

The list below is not an exhaustive list but is sufficient enough to get you started down the path of creative financing. Let's get started.

All Cash

The king of all financing tactics is the all-cash deal. Remember that cash is king, and in real estate it truly is. If there are two offers for a seller to consider and one is all-cash and the other is using conventional financing, the seller will usually go with the all-cash deal. This is because cash is quick, clean, and there are no banks to deal with that could get in the way of closing the sale of property. The all-cash deal is very attractive to sellers because it's the easiest form of financing tactics available.

Honestly, this is a great way to buy properties if you have the money, but it is not the best way for a return on your investment (ROI). As you saw in Day 7, using leverage and putting as little money out of your pocket down to buy the property, brings you the highest return. The deal in Day 7 shows that with only $10,000 down you can get a 780% return on your investment in just the first year! Now if you had paid for the property all cash your return would have been only 78% because you put $100,000 down to buy the property instead of only $10,000. The less you put down for the property, the higher your return rate will be.

Conventional Mortgage

Using a mortgage on a property means to get a loan from a bank who pays the purchase price minus the down payment you put towards the property. So if you buy a home for $100,000, and put $10,000 down, the loan you have is $90,000 that you will make payments on every single month until the balance is paid off. The bank does this because they get interest on the money they lend you. Most conventional mortgages for an investment property require a minimum of 20% down payment, and some can even ask for 25% to 30% depending on the lender you are working with.

Conventional mortgages usually have the lowest interest rate of all types of financing available. There are many term lengths to choose from: 10 year, 15 year,20 year, and 30 year. The longer the term in length, the more money you pay in total interest, but the lower your payments will be. See the chart to understand how you pay most of your interest up front in the first half of the term of the loan. In the beginning, only 15% or so of your monthly payment goes towards the principal and 85% goes to interest. Over time, the payment percentages change and eventually meet in the middle. At the end of the loan, you are basically paying the principal balance of the note. Needless to say, the banker makes his money at the beginning of the note and wants you to refinance again to start the payment schedule all over again.

FHA Loans

FHA loans are loans from the Federal Housing Administration which is a department of the United States government who insures mortgages for banks. The banks basically get insurance on the money they lent you to purchase your home. An FHA loan is strictly for owner occupied properties and not meant for investment properties. The benefit of these types of loans is the low down payment which is usually 3.5% of the purchase price. Considering a conventional mortgage is a minimum of 20%, you are able to pay a much lower down payment to get into a house. This is attractive because it means you will have a higher rate of return because you put less money down on the property.

Even though the FHA loan is for owner occupied only, there are ways to use this for your benefit of investment properties. Say you buy one property to live in with an FHA loan. You can then refinance the loan after one to two years to get out of the FHA loan. After that, you can then buy a second home with a new FHA loan and rent out the first. You can also use this FHA loan to buy a duplex, triplex, or four-plex if you plan on living in one of the units and renting out the others.

There are negatives to this type of loan, though. Each person can only have four total loans before FHA will not allow you to use them many more. That means after you have four homes with a mortgage on them, you will not be able to purchase another home with an FHA loan. Another negative is that included in every month's mortgage payments is a charge called Private Mortgage Insurance (PMI). This is the payment you pay for the bank's insurance on the money the lent you. You are basically making an insurance payment just like you would your car insurance or health insurance, but it goes to the FHA department for insurance in case you default on loan. Only after you have 20% home equity in the property will this FHA PMI have the ability to go away. That has usually been the case, but there are new laws that potentially make the FHA PMI permanent and may never go away until you refinance the home into a non-FHA loan.

Portfolio Lenders

Most banks who lend on conventional loans do not lend their own money but use other sources to fund the loan from a third-party. Even after the banks acquire a loan, they usually sell (for a profit) that loan to government-backed institutions like Freddie Mac and Fannie Mae in order to get their money back so they can do it all over again. Some banks and credit unions lend from their own funds on properties which makes them a portfolio lender because the money is their own institutions money. Because the bank's lending their own money on the portfolio note they are able to have more flexible terms and qualifying standards for each loan. Not many banks actually do portfolio lending but if you do a search on the Internet you may be able to find a portfolio lender to help you purchase a property.

Owner Financing

Another way to finance properties is to have the homeowner be the bank. The deal would be to have the homeowner hold the note against the property just like a bank would if they lent you money to buy the property. If the seller is in a position where they can hold the note, you would negotiate with them the terms and interest rate just like you would with a bank. Obviously, the lender is the homeowner and would have his own requirements for you like a down payment, interest rate, terms, balloon payment, and other requirements that he may come up with.

It is only worthwhile to you as an investor to do owner financing if one of two things are true: the seller owns the property free and clear, or the mortgage that he has on the property is an assignable loan. The former is where the owner does not have any outstanding mortgages on the home and owns the property outright. The latter is a loan that the owner can sign his rights and obligations over to you as the buyer and the mortgage company will now see you as the homeowner and note holder taking his place.

It's not advisable to purchase a home with owner financing if there is a mortgage on the property that cannot be assigned because most mortgages have a "Due on Sale" clause. This is a way for the banks to protect themselves by calling in the note immediately when there is a change of ownership on the property. If the full balance of the note cannot be paid, the lender has the ability to foreclose on the property and take the property away from you. Some investors don't mind the risk and buy the property subject to the other loan and risk the bank foreclosing on the property. I have seen how other investors have done this, and it seems like as long as the mortgage payments are being paid the bank doesn't concern themselves because the note is still current.

Owner financing may be one of the best ways to get a property with little or no money down because the owner is in control and not a bank. You don't have to worry about lenders, underwriters, or any other potential hang-ups stopping you from getting the property.

Hard Money

A hard money loan is a type of loan from a private business or individual that you can obtain to invest in real estate. This term sounds scary at first glance because one may think of a Mafia gangster named "Jimmy the Wolf" with a baseball bat ready to bust your knees if you don't pay. This is just not the case, but you should also stay away from "Jimmy the Wolf" for health reasons.

Hard money has many advantages over other forms of financing but does have some drawbacks. Some benefits include: no income verification, no credit references, the deal can be funded in a couple days,the loan is based on the value of the property after repairs are done, and you can have the rehab costs included in the loan. The drawbacks are: short-term notes (6 months to 3 years), much higher interest rates (15% or more), more loan fees to obtain the loan (points).

Before you get a hard money loan, make sure that you have multiple exit strategies so you don't get caught between a rock and a hard place and lose lots of money. Some exit strategies may be where you fix and flip the property and make a profit when you sell the property and pay back the hard money loan. Another would be to refinance the property after six months to a conventional mortgage with longer terms and lower interest rate.

Even though there are some drawbacks to a hard money loan, hard money can be a very effective way of making money in real estate if you do it right. In order to find hard money lenders, check the internet and talk to real estate agents for references.

Private Money

Private money is a loan from anyone who will lend it to you. It can be your mother, your uncle, your college roommate, even the shopkeeper down the street. This is basically a relationship loan because of the credibility you have built up with the individual lending you money. If you have proven yourself trustworthy and have integrity, you may be able to present a deal that you are working on to one of these private parties and bring them in as an investor. The benefit for them is they will get a higher rate of return than they would in a savings account by receiving interest oon the money lent to you. The interest rate and terms are up to you to negotiate with them, and they basically become the bank for you.

A private lender is solely there to lend you money with interest and usually does not take equity in the deal nor cash flow from the property. That means that you own the property outright, and all cash flow is yours minus the note payment you pay the private investor. The goal is to take the money from the private investor, much like you would with a hard money lender, buy a property, and then refinance out the money you borrow from the lender. Now you will hopefully have a conventional mortgage on the property at a lower interest rate and longer terms.

A way to find private money is to let everyone you know and meet that you are a real estate investor. This can be from casual conversations like "What do you do for living?" You can answer simply, "I am a real estate investor who invests in rental properties that give a passive income each month in cash flow." Your honesty and integrity are your calling cards when you search for private money. If people see you as someone they cannot trust, they will not lend you any money because they don't believe that you will pay them back.

Home Equity Loans and Lines of Credit (HELOC)

If you currently own a home you may have equity buildup in the property that you can use to purchase more rental properties. A home equity loan is basically a loan against the equity that you currently have in the property. These types of loans do not normally exceed 80% of the value of your home, but if you have enough equity in the property it can be a very good way to purchase more rentals.

For example: If you own a home that is worth $200,000, and you only owe $70,000, you would be able to borrow up to 80% of the $200,000 minus the original note of $70,000. 80% of $200,000 is $160,000. Subtract the $160,000 by the amount you currently owe ($70,000) and you have $90,000 left to borrow from your equity. A good way to use this loan would be to purchase a $90,000 property that will make you money each month from the rents and use that money to pay the mortgage payment each month. A mortgage payment of $90,000 may be around $650 a month, and you can buy a property that rents for $1000 giving you a profit of $350 month cash flow. This new rental property is now free and clear to get another home equity loan on and do it all over again.

A home equity line of credit (HELOC) is similar to a Equity Loan but the only difference is that the HELOC is a revolving line of credit like a credit card. With a HELOC you can borrow money against the equity on your home and then pay it off at any given time so as to not incur any interest if the balance is zero. The small annual fees that you incur having the HELOC are minimal compared to the value that it brings you to have money at your fingertips ready for the next deal.

Partnerships

A partnership is like a loan from a private investor, but instead of getting a monthly note payment, the investor gets equity in the deal. That means the investor owns a portion of the property and likewise a portion of the income and expenses. The equity stake the investor takes in the partnership is all negotiable and should be discussed when presenting the deal. The equity portion is usually based on the total cash invested from each party to the total cash invested as a whole for the deal. The major benefit with a partnership is economies of scale. All parties involved bringing money into the deal and can buy a larger building, apartment complex, or whatever type of deal you were going to purchase. It is called synergy. Synergy is the creation of a whole that is greater than the sum of its parts.

I'll give you an example from my experience with other investors I work with. Separately, each investor has a small amount of money to put towards a property, but together we all combine our money and have the ability to buy a much larger apartment complex. If each of three investors brings $50,000 into the deal, then we will have a total of $150,000 for the purchase. On a commercial loan for an apartment complex the minimum down payment is 20%, so the ability to buy a property works like this:

Individual	Partnership
Duplex with $1,600 monthly rent	18 Unit Apartment with $8,000 monthly rent
Total Purchase Price: $250,000	Total Purchase Price: $750,000
20% Down payment: $50,000	20% Down Payment: $150,000

For an individual, $50,000 is 20% of $250,000 and can possibly by you a duplex or a triplex. With a partnership, $150,000 is 20% of $750,000 and can buy a small apartment complex with 15 or more units depending on the area. The rent to price ratio has increased, as well as the price per door has gone down. With the duplex, you pay $125,000 per door, but with a partnership the per door cost is $42,000. As you can see, the purchasing power of a partnership will allow you to buy a much larger property with more monthly rent.

There is much more to learn about partnerships and investing in multi-family properties, but this might just whet your appetite to learn more about it. The goal of any investor in rental properties should be to progress into apartment complexes because that is where the money truly is. There are many things to learn from single-family homes before you should attempt to move into multi-family apartments. Start with single family homes first and progress in properties as your skills progress.

Putting All the Financing Together

As you can see, there are many different ways to finance properties, and this list is just a few of them. Again, your role as a real estate investor is to find creative ways to purchase rental properties and work hard to not use your own money if it all possible. Because each deal is totally different depending on the circumstances of the seller, it is difficult to say which method is the best. What you can do is try to understand each method and learn how to apply them to each deal so that you will be ready when the deal comes.

STRUCTURING YOUR DEAL

In the process of acquiring properties, making the offer is probably the most nerve racking thing you will encounter. Do your best to push yourself through it and get the offer on the table. Like all things that get easier the more you do it, presenting an offer is no exception. What it comes down to is if you are meeting the needs/desires of the seller and are creating a win-win transaction. It may be good to practice presenting the offer to someone you know and would be able to get feedback on how you do.

Try your best to stay calm when you are presenting the offer to the seller but don't worry if you are nervous. Nerves are a good thing to have and can keep you humble. People do not really like cocky or arrogant people and if you stay humble and helpful, you will get a lot more deals done because of your attitude.

Depending on how you structure you offer, it needs to be written in a way that the seller will accept it even though it is a lower amount than they are asking for. The price you are going to offer is based on the numbers you calculate from the income and expenses of the property.

Let's look at the property on 321 Main St. for this example with the $100,000 asking price.

Monthly Expenses	Monthly Income
Mortgage: $536 (5% note at 30 years)	Rents Collected: $1100
Taxes: $100	Net Operating Income (NOI): ($1,100-$175)=$925
Insurance: $75 **Total Monthly Expenses: $711**	**Total Profit (Income - Expenses): $389**

For the income on this property, check with one of the PM's you have been working with to get an estimate of what the property would rent for. You can also look through www.zillow.com and www.craigslist.com to do your own research to find the rental estimates.

For the Expenses, find all fixed expenses for the property that you, as the owner, must cover. This would be everything other than the utilities, water, sewer, garbage, yard maintenance etc. All these things, the tenant will be responsible for unless your lease is written in a way that has you paying for these items. (I never pay these). There are really only a few expenses you will have.

1. Mortgage

If you are going to use leverage by acquiring a note on the property, you will need to calculate the total monthly payment. You can use my free mortgage calculator to get this number.

http://www.masterpassiveincome.com/investment-calculators/mortage-calculator/

Remember that you may have Private Mortgage Insurance if you use an FHA loan to acquire the property which will increase the monthly payment.

2. Real Property Taxes

The County Tax Collector will have the current rent roll for the property. Most counties have the ability for you to look the information up online. Once you have the total annual taxes, divide that number by twelve to see how much money per month you will have to save. You will either hold onto this money in a savings account or put the money in an impound account with the mortgage company who will pay the taxes on your behalf with your money. Either way, make sure to save this money from each month's rent so you do not get hit with a tax bill you do not have the money for.

3. Homeowners Insurance

Contact your insurance agent to see what the cost of insurance would be for the property you are looking at. Just like with the taxes, divide the annual cost by twelve to calculate the monthly amount you are to save or put into the impound account with the taxes. If you are concerned about how to set up an impound account, don't be. You actually don't do a thing other than tell the mortgage company you would like one set up, and they will do all the work. It will be more common that the impound account for the insurance and taxes would be required by the mortgage company. This protects the bank because they will be sure that the taxes and insurance are being paid.

4. Homeowners Association

Depending on the area you are investing in, there may be a homeowners association that you are required to join and pay money into. I personally don't like homeowners associations and stay away from properties that have them. That is my personal preference. I feel that these associations just take money out of your pocket and dictate to you what you can do with YOUR property. Anyways, this is something to consider in your expenses.

5. Governmental Fees for Rental Properties

This is another expense that depends on where you are investing in. There are some cities and counties that require a rental inspection of the property to make sure the home is in livable condition. The cost usually is not too high (around $50 per year) but you must account for every expense so you can be prepared for everything.

I feel this is a fee just to make the government more money. I have found the free market to be the best way to keep business honest. If the property is not in livable condition, no one will live there. If they did, the rent would be so cheap because of the living conditions. Oh well, the government passed the law and now we have to pay. Make sure you have your fees paid. If you don't the government will never leave money on the table and never wait to penalize you. You could owe 10 times as much in penalties than the fees would have cost you. Trust me, I know from experience... ☹

6. Vacancy Allowance

The Vacancy Rate is a numerical value calculated as the percentage of time, per year, the property will be vacant. When the property is vacant, you do not make any money. If you believe the average amount of time a unit will be vacant for the area you are investing in is one month per year, calculate the rate as a percentage and subtract that from your income.

For an example:
A property that rents for $1,100 and is potentially vacant 1 month out of the year, the vacancy rate would be 8%.1 month vacant / 12 months in a year =.08

The total monthly income for the property would be $1,100 – (1,100*8%) = $1,012 per month income from the rents. Basically, you are subtracting one month's rent from the annual rent total and dividing it by the number of months in the year. Now plug this number into your valuation to see how the numbers turn out.

This is a good expense to plan for because you may need it or not. If you are blessed enough to not have a vacancy in the year, then your profits rise considerably. But if you do have a vacancy in the year, you are ready for it.

7. Capital Reserves

This expense is in case anything happens to your property unexpectedly like a roof leak, water heater replacing, or an HVAC systems need to be repaired. You are basically saving for a rain day fund where you will be able to draw money from when you need it. It is a huge headache having to repair or replace something on your property but you add insult to injury if you do not plan for how you are going to pay for it. I recommend saving 10% of the income each month for these expenses until you save up one and one half of one month's rent. For the property that rents for $1,100, save 10% each month until you have $1,650 saved up for a rainy day. Remember, this is your money and is yours until you need it. If you sell the property, this money is yours to do with whatever you want.

Now take all this information you have collected about the income and expenses and use my Rental Cash Flow Calculator to see if the property will make you money each month or not. I did all the hard work so you do not. Just put in the numbers you have and the calculator will do the valuation for you. www.masterpassiveincome.com/resources/

You can play with the numbers you put in so you can find the price you actually may want to offer. For starters, use the asking price to see what type of cash flow you will get from the property. Then you can adjust the number down until you get the total dollar amount per month that you are looking for. I personally like to get over $250 per "Bread and Butter" property if I am to invest. Anything less makes the margins too tight and may end up costing you in the long run. **Remember that you make your money when you BUY**

the property and realize your money when you SELL the property.

One way to quickly find a price for the property is to use my 70% Rule calculator on my site: www.masterpassiveincome. com/resources/

This calculator will take the AFTER Repair Value, minus repair costs and profit you desire from the deal and find the purchase price. This will give you a ball park figure to start with in your numbers. By no means should this be used as your only way to value a deal but it does get you started in the right direction. If you did purchase this property, you would already have the repairs and desired profit already built into the offer price.

Private Sellers

If you are working with a private seller, you can present many different offers. One would be with conventional financing,another with seller financing, and another can be a blend of the two. The conventional financing offer would generally be a lower offer price for the property because of the costs involved with the financing. With Seller financing, the owner is the bank and your job is to sell them on how much money they will make if they are to carry the note on the property and make interest from the property.

Conventional Financing Offer: If you go to a bank for conventional financing of a rental property, they will require you to put down at least 20% of the purchase price ($100,000*20%=$20,000) and will give you financing for the rest. Depending on your credit, your interest rate may be higher or lower which adjusts your monthly payment and total cost for the property.

Use the Investment Property Calculator to find your desired total monthly cash flow by adjusting the purchase price. Since the calculator works seamlessly, you can adjust the purchase price to see how much your total monthly cash flow will be. Since you are trying to replace your income with passive income in rental properties, making your offers based on the cash flow amount will help benefit you to quit your job. There are other ways to value a property but this is the Master Passive Income way.

Example: Offer price: $85,000

20% Down Payment: $17,000 Total Loan Amount: $68,000 Rate: 5% Term: 180 months **Monthly Payment: $538**	Insurance: $75 Taxes: $100 Mortgage Payment: $538 **Total Monthly Expenses: $713**

Monthly payment: $538 + Expenses of $175 = $713 per month

Rent of $1,100 – Total Expenses of $763 = $387 per month CASH FLOW!

Seller Financing Offer: You can offer the seller their full asking price of $100,000 with him holding the note as if he were the bank. You can ask for a no interest loan from him for the property and pay him the asking price over 15 years.

He would benefit because he is getting his full asking price which is $15,000 more than he would get if you were to get your own financing. You will pay $556 per month which is a little more than you would pay for a note but you have no money down which would make this deal have an infinite rate of return because no money comes out of your pocket. You can find a sample addendum to use with your offer in my resources section of my site. Owner Financing Addendum

Example: Offer price: $100,000

0% Down Payment: $0 Total Loan Amount: $100,000 Rate: 0% Term: 180 months **Monthly Payment: $556**	Insurance: $75 Taxes: $100 Mortgage Payment: $556 **Total Monthly Expenses: $781**

Monthly payment: $556 + Expenses of $175 = $731 per month payment

Rent of $1,100 – Total Expenses of $731 = $369 per month CASH FLOW with NO MONEY DOWN!

If you present both of the offers to the seller, you give them the option to choose what he desires. Plus you benefit because the seller can give you an idea of the type of deal he is looking for. Since the cash flow for each of the deals is the same, they are basically the same deal other than one big factor. The seller financing option does not require any money out of your pocket in order to get the deal. The seller financing deal like this example is less common and would take some work to find. This example is to show that you, as an investor, need to be creative in finding the right type of financing in order to get the deal. You don't know what the seller will choose in the end, or if he will choose at all so present the offers to at least give him the choice.

You can also get creative and blend the two types of offers together into another offer. Let's us the same example property with a purchase price of $100,000 and use both seller and conventional financing. For this property, you do not have the 20% down payment for the full asking price, nor do you have any money for the deal. No problem! Blend these two together like this:

Blended Offer #1: You need a mortgage for the bulk of the loan and you need another for the down payment. Offer the seller full asking price for the property in exchange for him to assist with the down payment. By having the seller take a note for $20,000 for the 20% purchase price of the property you now have the down payment covered. So, you effectively have a conventional note for $80,000 and a second note from the seller for $20,000 and you have no money in the deal.

Example: Offer price: $100,000

Conventional Financing 20% Down Payment: Paid by Seller Total Loan Amount: $80,000 Rate: 5% Term: 180 months **Monthly Payment: $632**	Seller Financing No Down Payment Total Loan Amount: $20,000 Rate: 0% Term: 180 months **Monthly Payment: $111**	Insurance: $75 Taxes: $100 Note Payments: $556 **Total Monthly Expenses: $918**

Monthly Conventional payment: $632 + Seller Payment: $111 + Expenses of $175 = $918 per month

Rent of $1,100 – Total Expenses of $918 = $182 per month CASH FLOW with NO MONEY DOWN!

Blend Offer #2: In this offer, you will have the seller finance the bulk of the loan and get conventional financing for the smaller portion. Offer the seller full asking price of $100,000 for the property and have him take a $65,000 note while the conventional financing would be for the remainder of the balance of $35,000. Like the blended offer, you will not have to come up with the down payment because the mortgage company does not require it and you can talk your seller into a zero down deal. Now, you have a conventional note for

$35,000 and a second note from the seller for $65,000 and you still have no money in the deal.

Example: Offer price: $100,000

Conventional Financing 0% Down Payment: $0 Total Loan Amount: $35,000 Rate: 5% Term: 180 months **Monthly Payment: $277**	Seller Financing No Down Payment Total Loan Amount: $65,000 Rate: 0% Term: 180 months **Monthly Payment: $361**	Insurance: $75 Taxes: $100 Note Payments: $638 **Total Monthly Expenses: $813**

Monthly Conventional payment: $277 + Seller Payment:$361 + Expenses of $175 = $813 per month

Rent of $1,100 – Total Expenses of $813 = $287 per month CASH FLOW with NO MONEY DOWN!

With these different offers, you can see that there are many different ways to get creative with the deal and try to make the deal work for both you and the seller. Try to make a win-win in all situations. If you find the seller needs to have steady income into his retirement years, seller financing may be the best option. If he needs the cash now in order to move to a new location, then help him get as much cash as possible within your already calculated valuation. Remember to never do a deal that will lose you money in cash flow.

Dealing with a Realtor

These same offers we worked on for a private party seller can also be presented through a Realtor as well. Think of a Realtor as a middle man who brings the offer to the seller. A down side of working with a Realtor in these types of deals is that Realtors want quick sales with as little work as possible. If the Realtors understand your deal, (big IF) then they may not want to take the time to present it to the seller because it is too much work. Legally the Realtor is supposed to present all offers but sometimes they do not.

Another downside is you may have to teach the Realtor how these deals work as well. Most Realtors are just salesmen who sell a product. That product is a home. Not a house, but a home. Most are not investors and just want to match up a buyer with a product they will buy and live in. They will tell you about the beautiful window coverings, nice lawn, etc. These are all useless to you as an investor. You know you are not going to live here and you are not buying the home for these reasons. You are buying the house for the cash flow of the property.

It is very easy to get your realtor's license and anyone is able to get one. Since you may be working with one of these types of Realtor's you may have some convincing to do on your part for her to present the offer, and present it well. It can be that you do your absolute best to create an offer that would work perfectly for the seller but the Realtor pitches it in such a horrible way that left the seller confused and possibly even mad. Be ready to put in extra work with a Realtor.

Buying from Bank

When you are buying from a bank, it is usually best to present as straight forward of an offer you can put together. If you have all cash, great, cut the asking price by a third and offer that. Banks are in the business of lending money not renting properties. The longer money sits in a property that no one is making a mortgage payment on, the more money they lose. That $150,000 property they foreclosed on is now a liability because of maintenance, taxes, security, etc. They want to get these off their books fast.

I have bought many properties from banks that had foreclosed on the previous owner because of non-payment. It is best to view banks as a business not a homeowner. Don't be concerned that you are hurting the banks feelings by offering as little as half the asking price. I purchase a property for 1/3 the asking price because the bank accepted the offer without a counteroffer. After 6 months from the offer date, the bank got back to me asking if the offer was still on the table. It was, so I bought the property and it has already paid me back in 2.5 years from the rents!

Writing the Contract

Now that you have some understanding of what types of offers you can give, check my resources page for sample contracts for you to use on your own deals. www.masterpassiveincome.com/resources. The Contract for Purchase is a quick and easy one for you to use on your first deal. If you are presenting multiple types of offers like we just talked about, fill out a new Contract for each offer you are presenting.

This all may seem daunting to you when you do it the first time. Don't let fear stop you from moving forward and putting in an offer on a property that will bring you passive income every month. Once you have one under your belt, it will get easier and easier. Tell yourself that you are a super investor and this is a walk in the park for you. Don't give up, push on through!

Taking Action for Phase 4.2:

Your action items for today are:

☐ *Continue searching through www.zillow. com and www.craiglist.com for more properties. Make it a habit to be looking for properties in everyday. You need to learn and know your market in order to know what a good deal looks like.*

☐ *Look through the Resources Page on my website: www.masterpassiveincome. com/resources. Here, you will find calculators to value single family homes and multi-family apartments, landlord deals, suggested books, and much more.*

You have just completed Phase 4.2and are ready to get out there and get the business started. Keep going through this eBook because you will be given step by step, the instructions to find and buy your first rental property.

PHASE 5 –GET TO WORK!

PHASE 5.1: YOUR 7 WEEK STEP-BY-STEP PROCESS TO ACQUIRE YOUR FIRST RENTAL PROPERTY

In this last phase, you are going to go through the process of finding your first rental property step-by-step. Just think, in seven weeks you may have your first rental property and have passive income to replace your income and quit your job! Each week, you are going to have action items to complete. If you follow the steps properly, you will acquire your first rental property. For the next seven weeks, you must commit to being an investor in rental properties and commit to following each of the action items.

As I've said earlier in the book, this is going to take time and it doesn't happen overnight. This is not a get rich quick scheme but is a way to build lasting wealth for you and your family. Be patient and diligent in doing all the action items and do your best. As you are looking for properties and building your business, you are also getting valuable experience that will help you get better at this business. They say that knowledge is power but I believe applied knowledge is truly power. Take what you've learned through this eBook and apply them to your next seven weeks so you too can replace your earned income from your job with passive income from rental properties.

If you buy one property this year, two properties next year, three the following year, four the year after that, and in your fifth-year you buy five properties you will have 15 properties and have about $4000 in passive income. What if you kept buying more each year and continued to grow your rental business? Where could you be after 10 years, 15 years, or even 30 years? It is very likely that you could have over 100 rental properties and have a net worth of over $10 million!

I don't want you to get discouraged throughout this process because it does take patience. At times it might feel like it's going really slow, or it's hard to find a property. If you stick with it you will change your financial future forever and be financially independent. If there are periods of time when you have little to do on your rental business, use that time to focus on learning new ways to find properties and acquire them. Remember that your job as a real estate investor is to find deals, figure out ways to make the deal's work, and get creative with financing the properties. There are many deals to be made out there and it's up to you to jump on them and make them work for you!

Let's get started!

WEEK ONE - AREA RESEARCH

This week your job is to further learn your market around you. You have already researched properties online and now it's time to get out there and look at them physically. Try to block out 4 to 5 hours this week where you can drive the neighborhoods that you have identified as being a potential source of rental properties. You may already know the general layout of your city but this is all about seeing the actual properties that you are looking to buy. You need to get a good understanding of the neighborhoods, potential tenants, and properties that you're going to be investing in. Remember to be looking for the cookie-cutter home that you learned about in Phase 3.1.

A three bedrooms, two baths, two car garage, 1000 sqft or more single family home is the type of property that you're looking for. You'll probably see these in a tract home subdivision where all the properties look similar. This is where developers have created many properties from one large parcel that they broke up and built many individual properties in order to sell them for profit. These types of properties are exactly what you're looking for when you are starting your real estate rental business.

This first weekend, your job is to drive the neighborhoods around your home and take notes of what you see. Don't just drive the main streets, drive the side streets and look for ways to get into the subdivisions where these properties are located. Take note of any of these types of subdivisions you find on a map for future research that you can do online. Keep your eye out for any potential properties that are for sale or look neglected and may be an opportunity for you to buy.

This first week has really only one thing to do and that is get to know your market around you. Be sure to do this first week because it will help you in future weeks to be successful.

Action Items

- ☐ Printed a map of my city and marked the areas around me that I'm going to drive.

- ☐ Drive the areas around my city for 4 to 5 hours this week to find houses that meet my business model.

- ☐ Markdown all of the potential areas where tract homes and/or subdivisions that I will potentially invested.

- ☐ Research on www.zillow.com and craigslist.com the property values and rental estimates for these areas and make notes for future reference.

Week one is done and you are on your way to having passive income with rental properties so you can quit your job and be financially free!

WEEK TWO - MARKET RESEARCH

Great! It's the second week of your new business in rental properties. Take out your map and list of the neighbor-hoods you drove last week because we are going to put it to good use. This week you are to drive two to three of these neighborhoods and take more detailed notes on the neighborhood. Things to note are: for sale signs, vacant looking houses, age and condition of the homes and vehicles, how the properties are maintained, signs of children playing in the neighborhood, and try to find people to talk to in the area. Finding people to talk to might be one of the best ways to find out if this is a place where you want to invest. Nobody knows this area better than the people who live there and I've found that people enjoy talking about themselves as well as the place where they live.

You can invest in areas that are low class and not maintained very well but it is not advisable unless you are an experienced landlord. If you do, be ready to go through the school of hard knocks with problem tenants and evictions. It's not necessarily a bad idea to invest in low class neighborhoods but just be aware that it comes with many problems. I know firsthand about these types of neighborhoods because that's how I started investing. If you have the ability to, start investing in middle-class properties. You have a much easier time with tenants and have a more steady cash flow from your properties.

Look for how the homes are maintained and if the lawns are in good condition. This shows that there are homeowners or tenants who take pride in their neighborhood and community. Look for indications that families live in the neighborhood. Items like bicycles for kids, swing sets, jungle gyms, and other things children play with. In middle class neighborhoods, there should only be a few vacant homes in the area and this shows that the neighborhood is a desirable place for people to live in.

Look at how the people in the neighborhood live and if they take pride in the things they own or not. If there are rusted cars in the drive ways, overgrown vegetation, homes that are in disrepair, then this neighborhood may be a more rough area to invest in. If the vehicles are taking care of, lawns are manicured, and it feels like an enjoyable place to live, this may be the area that you are looking for. Neighborhoods like this are easier to rent and you get better tenants. You may even have neighbors around your property that will inform you if there any issues with your tenants.

When you're beginning investing in rental properties, you want to find the worst property in the best neighborhood. These properties will give you many benefits with owning them. If the neighborhood is desirable, you will have higher appreciation, rent amount may be higher, force the appreciation by the work you put into it fixing it up, and get better tenants because the value of the property is higher. Be on the lookout for these types of properties and make note of them. Whenever you find a property that is a bad home in a good area, write it down so you can keep track of it because it may come up for sale in the future.

Be on the lookout for people who you can talk to that live in the area. You may get a little nervous the first time you get out of your car to talk to somebody, but the more you do it the easier it will be. Just approach them with a smile and say that you're interested in buying a home in the area and wanted to know what they thought of the neighborhood, schools, the neighbors, and even the crime in the area.

Questions to ask somebody who is neighborhood

- if they live in the neighborhood

- what they like best about the area

- what they like the least about the area

- if there are any problems you should know about

- if there are any homes for sale that may be good deals

- ask about the neighbors and the people around them

- see if the majority of people own their homes or are rentals

- if they know anything about a property that you spotted down the street

Remember that people love to talk about themselves so just keep them talking about everything revolving around them. Ask questions, be polite, and thank them for their time and insight when you're done talking with them. Be sure to ask if they know of any properties that are for sale or have owners that are thinking about selling. Let them know that you are an investor and want to help people with quality places to live. You never know what they may tell you. You may even learn about someone who needs to sell their home quickly and you may be just the person to help.

If someone has gone through a divorce, lost their job, had other financial issues, and moving out of the area for whatever reason, you may be able to help them in the situation that they are in. They may need to sell the property quickly for cash or move out of the area and you are there to take care of their need. If you focus on the needs of the people you will be able to find better deals because you are finding ways to create a win-win situation and not take advantage of people.

Your goal should be to create a win-win situation for you and the seller in every deal you do. If you become known as an investor who cares about the people you buy from, people will be fine to work with you because of your reputation. Be honest and have integrity and all the dealings that you do with people.

Action Items

- ☐ Ride through three-four neighborhoods that you will potentially invest in.

- ☐ Speak to at least three people in each of the neighborhoods you're going to invest in.

- ☐ Ask each person if they know of any properties that are for sale in the area

- ☐ Try to find at least one property that's for sale the area and the owners information

- ☐ Search through Zillow.com and craigslist.com for other potential properties

- ☐ Contact the realtor that you have made a connection with to create an automated MLS notification for you when properties come on the market in that area with your specific criteria.

WEEK THREE - BUILD YOUR TEAM

To start this week you need to get out your list of property managers that you have already contacted and pick two of the managers you would like to work with. You are going to spend some time with these PM's getting to know them and the neighborhoods they would be managing. Block out at least two hours with each property manager and take them in the same areas but separately. You want to pick the brain of each of these managers to see what they know and what they don't know. This is basically an interview you are doing with them to see if they are the person you would want to spend your time and money with creating your business.

Have them talk about the neighborhoods you are driving, how their properties in the area are, how much they rent for, the type of tenants in the area, and any general information. Your goal is to get to know, them and the area, as well as specific properties. Take them to properties that you noted that are potential deals for you and ask them the estimated repair costs, rental rates, and other thoughts about the property. Since you are going with two different property managers at different times, be sure to ask similar questions to each so you can compare what they are saying about the property and neighborhood. Also get bids from them on how much a property would take to repair and get rented if you bought the property as is. If the difference between the two bids from each property manager is drastically different, take a third property manager along with you, through the same areas, asking the same questions, and having them give you a bid for the repairs for the properties. You will be able to compare all three and choose wisely of which property manager you're going to start your business with.

Ask the PM about the rental rates for a one-bedroom, two bedroom, and three bedroom homes in the area and make note of the rates they quote you. You will use these rates for your evaluation in the future. When you are asking the property managers for the rental rates for a particular property, make sure you specify that it should be for the after repair value not as is with the current condition. This will give you more accurate information when you run your numbers to make sure you know how much to offer for the property.

While you are interviewing the property managers for potential management of your properties, refer back to the section on what to look for in a property manager and the types of questions you should be asking them. A quick recap of the things to look for in a property manager is: trustworthiness, accountability, communication, quality of work, references, and commission percentage. As explained in this property manager section, make sure you find someone that fits all these qualities. I have walked away from entire areas of investing because I could not find a property manager with these qualities. Remember that when you hire a property manager, you are basically hiring an employee and it's up to you to hire the right employee for your business.

Now that you are more familiar with the area and a few particular property managers, you are armed with more information to help you be successful with investing in this area. Look through the classified ads, websites, MLS, and for sale by owner listings for other potential properties in the area. Make particular note of potential properties that you are interested in because we will begin to analyze them in week four.

Action Items

- ☐ Get to know the rental rates for the properties in the area by looking up current properties for rent on the Internet.

- ☐ Spend two hours with two separate property managers who will go on a ride along with you through the areas.

- ☐ Narrow down your list of potential properties to analyze and put offer on five properties.

- ☐ Find two-three for sale by owner properties that you will potentially pursue in these areas.

WEEK FOUR - LOOK AT PROPERTIES

This week you are going to get out and look at properties. It is now time to put all of this learning into action. Be sure to bring along one of the property managers that you selected as the one you will most likely do business with. Have him give you bids on these properties for all the repairs to make the property rentable. Since you have noted down two or three properties to evaluate, contact the owner or realtor inquiring of the property and scheduling a time to walk through the property. If you have a full time job, make it on the weekend which sellers will be fine to do. This will allow you to schedule the three properties close together to maximize your time with the property manager and not use up your entire day.

Each inspection should take about an hour and I suggest you use the property inspection checklist in the resources section of my website. www.masterpassiveincome.com/re-sources Be thorough with your inspection and take accurate notes of the condition of the property. You want to do your best to not have any surprises once you acquire the property, so take your time and do it right the first time. Have the property manager give you their thoughts of the condition of the major appliances, roof, foundation, and roofing of the property. It is important to have a checklist or a guide sheet that is going to help you to not miss anything as you are walking through the property.

You want to be looking for items that are in good, average, or poor condition. More than likely the items that are in good condition will not need to be repaired or replaced anytime in the near future. The items that are in average condition may need some repairs in the next 2 to 3 years. You can plan for these repairs in the future with a "repairs and maintenance" budget that you put into your numbers to be taken out of the rent each month. The items that are in poor condition will probably need to be replaced in short order and it will be wise to get the cost of repairing it and have that reflected in your offer price. If you don't know what the cost would be to replace an item don't be shy to get a vendor or general contractor to inspect the item and give you a bid to put into your numbers.

With all these numbers, they are just estimates that you are going to use and I suggest that you over estimate the costs rather than under. If you think a HVAC system is going to cost $2,500 to $5,000, put $5000 in your numbers as you are coming up with your offer price. It would be better to be surprised by having more money in your pocket because you over estimated than have a surprise that takes money out of your pocket because you didn't estimate properly. You may want to get a bid on replacing the roof of a property by calling a roofer and giving him the dimensions of the home to get a ballpark dollar amount for the repairs. Even though he will not give you an accurate bid you want to know what the maximum amount of cost will be. Remember to always be conservative on the high end when you're looking at these costs.

For all the little items like doorknobs, window trim, door casing, window screens, and any other minor repairs, use your best judgment to estimate a rough cost. Even if you do not account for half of these items properly, you will not break the bank. These are not big-ticket items that can cost you thousands like a roof or foundation problems. Just do your best to account for as much as you can. As you grow in experience you will be able to get more accurate with these estimates.

Action Items

☐ Review the Property Inspection Sheet on my website: http://www.masterpassiveincome. com/resources/forms-and-contracts/sf-rehab-inspection/

☐ Walk through three to four properties with the property managers to get bids from them for repairs to the property for your analysis of the deal.

☐ Fill out a property inspection sheet for each property you walk through for your notes and reference.

☐ Get rough estimates on the cost of any major repairs such as HVAC, roof, flooring, etc.

WEEK FIVE - ANALYZE THE NUMBERS

This week you need to refresh yourself on a couple of things in Phase 4.2. "Find the value of the deal" and "Making an offer on a property". This is very important because you are going to now be presenting multiple offers on the properties you have evaluated and you need to know how to do it. You will use the information from these sections to create your offer and not lose money on the property.

Don't worry about the asking price of the property because no matter what the seller is asking, the deal is only right for you when the numbers work in your favor. I once made an offer on a property that was a third the asking price and figured that I can work my way up from there and meet in the middle. After I submitted the offer I did not hear back from the bank to foreclose on the property for six months. After six months, I received a call from a realtor asking me if my offer was still on the table and that the bank would accept it as is. After I looked at the numbers again to make sure everything was the same I said yes and preceded to the buy the house for one third the asking price!

As always, you make your money when you buy the property and this is the point where you need to be extra diligent to make sure you buy the property at the right price. I personally do not get attached to any particular property and overpay because I run the numbers and stick to them. If you stick to the numbers and evaluate the property correctly you won't lose money.

Now you can't let it discourage you about the asking price and the appraisal value of the property because you do not buy properties at their appraised value. This is not a home you are going to live in, it is a place you will rent to a tenant. When someone is buying a home to live in they buy based on the market value of the property which is not what you're going to do. Don't listen to the appraiser, real estate agent, banker, seller, etc. because they are not investors. You are an investor and you only buy properties that are good investments.

I always offer less than my maximum purchase price so I have the ability to negotiate a counter offer and work my way up. You should always know what the maximum purchase price should be for a deal and always stop there. Never fall in love with a property and overpay. There are plenty of properties out there for you to make more offers on. Now there are times when I do present my full maximum offer to start with because of outside circumstances. If it is a seller's market and there are many offers coming in, I present the best offer because I do not want to lose the property by trying to low-ball them. If a property is on the market for over 30 days then you should have the ability to negotiate the price of the property down.

The goal of your investing is to make cash every month from the rent less all expenses. Use my rental property cash flow calculator on my website to help you find the value of the deal and the cash flow every month you will receive. http://www.masterpassiveincome.com/resources/investment-property-calculators/

When you complete your valuation of the property and know what you're going to offer, the next step is to present the offer to the seller. I personally use a real estate agent to write and present all my offers. If you want to present an offer yourself, check out the forms and contracts section on my website for sample contracts and forms for you to use as a template for your deals that you present. http://www.masterpassiveincome.com/resources/forms-and-contracts/

Now that you are ready to present your offers on the properties that you have evaluated, put all fears aside and present your offers to the seller's. What's the worst that could happen? They say no right? The best thing that could happen is they say yes to your offer and you have a great property at a great price. Don't be afraid to present the offers or have your realtor do so. Everyone feels nervous or anxious about presenting their first offer, but the more offers you present the easier it will become.

Action Items

- [ ] Review phase 4.2 Find the value of the deal
- [ ] Review phase 4.2 Making an offer on a property
- [ ] Use the Rental Property Cash Flow Calculator and find the value of each property you evaluated

☐ Present offers on at least three properties

WEEK SIX - NEGOTIATING AND COUNTERING

This week you have two things to do. One, review all counter offers you receive. Two, find for more properties to put offers on.

Reviewing offers you receive should be fairly quick and easy since all the hard work has been done already. If the seller has countered with a lower asking price, then put that number in your numbers and see if the deal works for you. If it does, great jump on the property. If it does not then make a counter offer and raise your offer price by 1% to 3% of the original offer if your numbers still work at that price. This may become somewhat of a dance where you and the seller go back and forth with counter offers. I have had some offers take four to five counter offers before we settled on a price.

Just like in week four, your job is to go out and look for more properties to put offers on. Follow the steps in week four to find other properties to evaluate. Don't worry so much about finding a new area for properties at this point because the current area you are working in probably has enough inventory to last you a few months of offers.

This is a numbers game. The more offers you make, the better your chances are getting an accepted offer and buy your first property. It may be that it takes 10 offers before you buy one, but if you buy it right that one property will be worth all the work you put in to acquire it. Do not get impatient at this point. Most of the work has already been done and you are so close to the end. Finding your first property is just the start of a long career in investing in rental properties and you need to be persistent if you want to win this game.

Action Items

- ☐ Review phase 4.2 Find the value of the deal and Structuring The Deal again to memorize how the valuation works.

- ☐ Use the Rental Property Cash Flow Calculator and find the value of each property you evaluated

- ☐ Present offers on at least three more properties

WEEK SEVEN - REVIEW AND REPEAT

You may see a pattern now start to emerge this week. You are going to go out and evaluate more properties that are for sale. It can be either a For Sale by Owner (FSBO) property or one that is on the MLS and is listed by a realtor. Remember that the more offers you put in, the more chances you get to purchase your first property. If you don't put in an offer the seller has nothing to consider and you miss out on a property. Don't let indecision or procrastination keep you from starting down the path of passive income in rental properties.

Because you are an investor, a lot of your offers will be passed on because of the price you are willing to pay for the property. Don't let that bother you. Each "no" you receive is one closer to the "yes" that will get you your first property. Be looking through all of the ways we discussed how properties are listed and keep looking for properties.

Always be conscious of the rent amount that you will be able to get out of the property once you have the rehab completed. Rents fluctuate from time to time but usually do not go down very much. Once you have an understanding of the potential rent for a property you will know if the property will produce a cash flow for you are not.

Remember this is a numbers game, and the more offers you put in the more likely you are to get one. Review again the section on finding the value of the property so you have that in your head as you're walking through properties. After time, you will begin to see a property and tell within five minutes if it's a property worth pursuing are not.

Repeat the steps outlined above until you successfully purchase a property. Once you have this one rented and are ready to buy another, go out there and put more offers on more homes. Over time, you will have created a large portfolio of rental properties that will help you quit your J.O.B because you have enough passive income through rental properties.

WHAT YOUR LEARNED

I n this eBook we've covered how to become a rental property investor from beginning to end.

In Phase 2.1, we went through basic training about how to get your life in order. You must commit to self-education and find out who you are financially and create a budget so you can save for the future.

In Phase 2.2, we looked at why you should invest in rental properties with the four ways rental properties make you money: monthly cash flow, equity, appreciation, and tax advantages. We also saw how you can create equity three different ways; by reducing debt, making money when you buy a property, and forced appreciation through rehab. We also looked at how rental properties have 11 other fantastic reasons to invest in them.

In Phase2.3, we learned how to think like a rich person, and how traditional education is teaching you the way of an employee, not the way of an investor. We saw how we do not want to trade hours for dollars anymore but want to be paid for the value that we bring. We learned about the cash flow quadrant and how it is best to be in the investor quadrant investing in real estate rental properties.

In Phase 3.1, we learned how to make our money work for us and have our dollars be like little employees working for us all day every day. You also learned about how to quit your job by using rental properties to create passive income.

In Phase 3.2, we looked at the long process of understanding the mechanics of a transaction in the buying process of a rental property.

In Phase 4.1, we learned about how to create our real estate business dream team. From property managers to contractors, having a team is the most vital part of your business. This is a team sport and no one can do it alone.

In Phase 4.2, we learned how to get started with rental properties and how to find properties, evaluate them, and to find the value in the deal. We also talked about how to determine if the property cash flows.

Phase 5.1 took you step-by-step through the process of acquiring your first rental property. If you followed the steps outlined, and continue to be persistent, you WILL find your first rental property. Don't give up, keep going. It will get easier and easier as you get more experience and get to know more people.

YOUR NEXT STEPS

You are now done with all the phases in this eBook and hopefully on your way to your first property. Thank you so much for taking part in my eBook and I hope you the best in your investing carrier. As you can possibly see, we have only just scratched the surface on how much more there is to learn. Even though you reached the end of this eBook, you are just at the beginning of the rest of your life with passive income in rental properties.

Now that you have finished the Quit Your Job with Passive Income in Rental PropertieseBook you should have a good understanding of how to get out there and start your investing career in rental properties. This is only the beginning of an amazing journey ahead of you. There is much more to learn about rental properties and how to create passive income through real estate and www.masterpassiveincome. com is here to help you be successful with rental properties. If you have questions, issues, roadblocks, or even need some advice, I am here to help you in any way that I can.

Remember that all of this is just a mindset that anyone can develop, including you. Just like me, you have been trained all your life through government education about how to be an employee. It takes time to change how you look at yourself from simply being an employee to becoming an investor. Right now, you are an investor. Tell yourself that every day when you wake up–you are a successful real estate investor in rental properties–because it is true. You now have the knowledge the resources to help you be successful.

I want you to be a part of the Master Passive Income community along with all the others who are in the same place as you. You can ask me questions directly, work with others on the forum section, and possibly even get on the podcast with your questions. Let me help you with your investing and be able to quit your job with rental properties!

For further learning, go to www.masterpassiveincome.com and go through the blogs, podcasts, and resources which are designed to help you invest in your own education. And it is ALL FOR FREE! My blog and podcast is full of free knowledge and information for you to learn and grow from. Please check out my website for loads of free information on how to be a successful rental property investor.

Sign up for my newsletter where I will send you exclusive content that you won't find anywhere else on my blog. I value your time and will only send you things that will benefit you in your investing carrier.

For signing up, I'll send you exclusive content about creating a real estate business that you will not see anywhere else.

www.masterpassiveincome.com is here to help you achieve the dreams and goals you have created for your life. Success breeds more success. Now is the time to act! Get out there, look at properties, analyze the deal, put in offers, and get started on your journey with Master Passive Income!

CONGRATULATIONS! YOU'RE DONE!

Let me know how you are doing and if you need any help, encouragement, or questions. I would love to help you quit your J.O.B with rental properties.

Send me an email: dustin@masterpassiveincome.com

If you enjoyed this book, please help spread the word by taking a moment and leaving an honest review in Amazon. Each rating will help us reach more people and help others quit their J.O.B. with rental properties.

DOWNLOAD THE AUDIOBOOK
AND PRINTABLE STARTER KIT FREE!

Just to say thank you for buying this book, we'd like to give you the full Audiobook of "How to Quit Your Job with Rental Properties" **100% FREE**

We'd also like to give you a printable PDF so you can print out the charts & tables included in the book.

DOWNLOAD FREE INSTANTLY HERE

http://www.masterpassiveincome.com/FreeAudioBook

70407401R10109

Made in the USA
Middletown, DE
13 April 2018